Industry Acclaim
Billing Power! and *The Recruiter's*
Almanac of Scripts, Rebuttals and Closes

"Billing Power is refreshing! I laughed, I remembered, I learned. It successfully repackages the basics and forces you back to preclosing excellence."
--- Peter D. Leffkowitz, International Trainer
President, Morgan Consulting Group, Inc.

*

"More than a comprehensive 'How to,' more than insightful money-making methodology, more importantly, Billing Power bursts with compassion, warmth and humor!"
--- Danny Cahill, CPC, International Speaker/Trainer

*

"Different than a training manual, Billing Power captures the true flavor of recruiting. I highly recommend it for everyone who is in the business, or is thinking of becoming a contingency recruiter."
--- Terry Petra, CPC, International Speaker/Trainer

*

"Billing Power made me feel proud of what I do and the service we provide...I thoroughly enjoyed this book, and will recommend it to all of our consultants."
--- Linda Krutzsch, VP Training and Operations
Accountants On Call, Inc.

*

"Right on target! The Recruiter's Almanac is readable, reliable, rational and respectable!"
--- Robert O. Snelling
Chairman, Snelling & Snelling, Inc.

*

"'Must' reading for everyone in our business. Insightful and informative, The Recruiter's Almanac is the best instructional manual of its kind!"
--- H. Brent Sanders, VP
Chase Adams, Inc.

*

"No office should be without The Recruiter's Almanac --- a perfect complement to Billing Power!"
--- Terry Petra, CPC
International Speaker/Trainer

Books and Tapes by Bill Radin

How to Market & Sell Your Recruiting Services
Innovative Consulting, Inc., 1999

How to Write High-Profit Job Orders
Innovative Consulting, Inc., 1999

Time Management Secrets
of Top-Producing Recruiters
Innovative Consulting, Inc., 1999

The Recruiter's Almanac
of Scripts, Rebuttals and Closes
Innovative Consulting, Inc., 1998

Recruiting & the Art of Control
How to Fill More Jobs in a Candidate-Driven Market
Innovative Consulting, Inc., 1997

Billing Power!
The Recruiter's Guide to Peak Performance
Innovative Consulting, Inc., 1995

Breakaway Careers
The Self-Employment Resource for
Freelancers, Consultants and Corporate Refugees
Career Press, 1994

Take This Job and Leave It
How to Get Out of a Job You Hate
and Into a Job You Love
Career Press, 1993

SHUT UP

and Make
More Money!

The Recruiter's Guide to
TALKING LESS
and BILLING MORE

By
Bill Radin

SHUT UP

&

Make More Money!

©1995 Innovative Consulting, Inc.
5193 Adena Trail, Cincinnati, Ohio 45230
Phone: (800) 837-7224 • Fax: (513) 624-7502
Email: billradin@aol.com • Web site: www.billradin.com

ISBN 0-9626147-3-4 • $49.95 Softcover
Cover Design: Anthony d'Agostino
Cover Photo: Terry Lynch
Editor: Betsy Smith
Printing: BookMasters, Inc., Mansfield, Ohio

10 9 8 7 6 5 4

Manufactured in the United States of America

Acknowledgments

The author wishes to thank those who helped make this book possible, including his family; plus all the dedicated professionals in the employment industry who offered me their wisdom and encouragement: Danny Cahill, Peter Leffkowitz, Paul Hawkinson, Bill Vick, Martin Yate, Tom Bloch, Jeff Allen, Bernie Frechtman, Bonnie Krstolic, Joe Ganim, Bob and Larry Cowan, Lou Scott, Alan Schonberg, Bob Snelling, Jim Gibson, Sandy Rose, Rick Keane, Linda Krutzsch, Michael Zatzick, Ron Farnham, Peter Yessne, Michael Schulman, Jim Lawson, Larry Nobles, Terry Petra, Phil Ross, David Lord, Andrea Kay and Joanne Must.

Also, thanks to Bill Moss, Kathy DeWitt, Betsy Smith, Tony D'Agostino, Terry Lynch, Bill Gwynne, Elaine Palin, Margie Hicks, Michael Herrick, Julie Hauck, Leslie Meaux-Druley, Eric and Lynn Oseas, Pat Codd, Ray Sevin, Scott Woelfel, Ken Kresge, Dorothy Rosa, Joe Ziomek, Dr. Kapur Kitay, Bill Zabriskie, and all the people at Kinko's and Alphagraphics for their preproduction support.

Shut Up and Make More Money!
Table of Contents

Table of Contents

Illustrations and Forms

Introduction: Talk Less, Earn More!

If you're in the recruiting business, you've probably been told a thousand times that the only way to make more money is to get on the phone --- and stay on the phone.

I beg to disagree! In fact, I want to show you how to selectively *hang up the phone* and dramatically increase your billings.

What nonsense, you're probably thinking. Since time began, recruiters have been taught that the number of phone calls we make directly translates into the amount of income we earn. *More calls, more money. More calls, more money.* It's the mantra we chant with our morning cappuccino.

Admittedly, recruiting has always been a telephone-based business. And for years, we've placed on a pedestal the tireless phone warriors who make two or three hundred outbound calls a day and put up the really big numbers.

With heroes like these, it's no wonder we obsess over "phone time" and "productivity," as if the two were inseparable.

What You Say and When You Say It

The truth is, phone time is only as valuable as you make it; in our line of work, there are easily as many poverty-level recruiters with big phone bills as there are monster producers. In other words, being born with the gift of gab never insured anyone of success.

The difference between high and low billers is tied to more than the sheer number of words spoken or the hours spent on the squawk box. Success or failure lies in the ability to control *what you say and when you say it*. The right amount of talk at the perfect time will work like magic; while too much talk at the wrong time will have an adverse effect on your business.

With respect to phone time, most of us simply don't have the stamina to wag our tongues twelve hours a day, 300 days a year, year after year. Could it be that we're lacking in motivation or doomed to a life of perpetual starvation? I don't think so. We simply burn out mentally or end up contracting a revolving case of laryngitis.

The Monkey at the Typewriter

My first boss once told me in a moment of confidence that he ascribed to the "monkey at the typewriter" theory of recruiting. That is, if you put enough monkeys behind a sufficiently large number of typewriters, then eventually one of them would write a passage from Shakespeare.

His point was that recruiters were just a different breed of monkey; and if he could find enough of them to yammer away on the telephone long enough, sooner or later they were bound to make placements.

Aside from the fact that he was telling this story to someone he considered to be a monkey, I found this concept offensive, and still do. It wasn't true then, and it certainly isn't now.

Sure, life on a desk is still a numbers game to a certain

14

extent, but as a veteran recruiter, trainer and manager, I can say with reasonable certainty that our business has evolved beyond the scope of a monkey, or any other *Sapien* armed only with a telephone and a strong set of lungs.

What's more, doing business in today's perplexing economy requires more training and sophistication than ever --- the market is too complicated, the candidates and employers are too savvy, and the competition is too keen for the weak or merely long-winded to survive.

Assimilation, Not Alteration

Which is exactly why I've written a modern approach to recruiting success. Like the title promises, *Shut Up and Make More Money* pays particular attention to verbal restraint and recruiter-specific business strategy.

Unlike a lot of get-rich recruiting methods, *Shut Up and Make More Money* provides you with techniques that can be quickly and painlessly incorporated into your overall approach, with no one asking you to change your market, your phraseology, your business ethics or the relationship you have with your constituency.

By utilizing the time- and voice-saving techniques in *Shut Up and Make More Money*, you'll be able to increase your productivity (and your earnings) by enhancing your efficiency both on and off the telephone.

The techniques described can easily be assimilated by any recruiter, in any size operation, contingency or retainer, regardless of industry focus; and they won't require you to drop everything you've done in the past or convert to a completely new method.

For example, you may decide to use marketing letters as a way to supplement, rather than replace cold calling as a means of reaching new prospects. Or, you may ask your clients to sign retained or partially retained contracts as opposed to signing off on contingency fee agreements, as a litmus test of their sincerity and commitment.

To PC or Not to PC

One of the major changes in our business over the last few years has been the emergence and proliferation of computers, fax machines, scanners, and information delivery systems such as on-line services, CD-ROMs and so forth. Without a doubt, these tools have demonstrated their amazing power to increase productivity and facilitate success.

However, I've deliberately avoided a discussion or endorsement of specific electronic hardware or software for two reasons: First, the technology is changing so rapidly that whatever I recommend will in all likelihood be obsolete or significantly re-priced a year from now.

Second, we each have our own individual threshold for digital absorption. The fact that you may or may not feel comfortable in front of a PC or have more or less computer literacy than another recruiter shouldn't affect your ability to succeed. As Forrest Gump's momma used to say, "stupid is as stupid does." A computer, fax modem or Internet address will only make a stupid recruiter more efficient at being stupid.

Using the Forms and Illustrations

To illustrate the power of written communications, I've included over 30 different examples of letters, contracts, promotional materials, resumes and survey forms. Let me point out that these are the *exact* materials that I use every day at my desk and with my clients and candidates. In certain cases, I've changed the names to protect the innocent (or condensed certain documents to fit on a smaller page). But I want to be clear that none of the examples have been watered down in an attempt to broaden their appeal or protect my flank.

Since I've copied the materials verbatim, you'll notice that some, especially the contracts, brochures and surveys, make reference to Radin Associates. My intent has nothing to do with ego and everything to do with inviting you to "get inside my head" and absorb whatever ideas you think would lend themselves to your own business development.

So feel free to copy or adapt the materials to whatever format you already use, whether it's a fancy computer system or plain old pen and paper. Just do me a favor and take the "Radin Associates" name off the contracts --- I have enough business without trying to fill *your* job orders, too!

Recruiting in the New Millennium

Throughout the book, I've blurred the line somewhat between the "contingency" and the "retained" aspects of recruiting. This is because so many of us have our feet in both worlds, and view success more as a function of getting the job done, not the method for getting paid.

In the next millennium, our business will necessarily evolve to meet the changing needs of candidates and employers; and like our constituency, we'll be faced with the innumerable challenges defined by an evolving employment marketplace.

By implementing even a few of the ideas in this book, I'm convinced you'll not only meet the challenges of the future and increase your billings as I have --- you'll also get a lot more pleasure out of running your business.

1

Sharpen Your Skills and Let the Good Times Roll

Bigger billings are achievable by any recruiter, no matter what your experience level, desk specialty or manner of fee generation. To begin the journey towards peak performance, it's important to recognize the four fundamental aspects of your business that are not only the cornerstones to success, but are also potentially ripe for improvement. These include your:

[1] *Verbal skills*. The more clearly you express your ideas (and learn to put a limit on verbiage that's counterproductive), the more you'll profit from daily activities such as marketing, negotiating, recruiting and closing.

[2] *Time management, planning and organization.* Since time is our only controllable commodity, it's always advantageous to implement whatever efficiency-enhancing methods are available.

[3] *Marketing communications.* The way your service is presented to new and existing clients is extremely important, both in terms of opening doors and maintaining profitable business relationships.

[4] *Control documents.* The intelligent use of written communications (for both internal and external consumption) will go a long way towards establishing your control over various situations. A signed contract specifying a delivery date for services, for example, will carry a lot more weight with an employer than an informal agreement.

Incremental improvements in any of these fundamental areas can do nothing but help your overall performance.

Look Before You Leap

The mere possession of fundamental skills, however, can only take you so far in a competitive business arena that's filled with nuance.

Imagine for a moment that you're a seven-footer who can slam dunk a basketball at will. You may have great NBA potential; but until you can learn to play the game, your contribution to the league will always remain limited.

By combining your fundamental skills with the ability to understand and play the game, you'll make great individual strides, and become an asset to your team, whether the team is your family, your associates, or your search organization.

To get a jump on the competition and play the game with maximum astuteness and consistency, let me suggest several time-tested techniques:

- **Conceptualize.** Before you begin an activity or a series of activities, you want to clearly understand the purpose behind what you're doing. For example, if you're going to spend the morning making marketing calls, you should formulate a specific list of primary goals you wish to achieve (such as a writing a workable job order or arranging a sendout), along with a list of secondary goals that might add to the value of the activity (such as gathering information about each target company, or building rapport with industry insiders to establish your credibility).

- **Strategize.** Work out in advance the tactics or logistics that are necessary to achieve your goals. Before you make recruiting calls, for example, you'll need to identify the appropriate talent pool, find the best way to reach candidates, and understand their motivational characteristics (or "hot buttons") in order to maximize your influence.

- **Prioritize.** Simply put, the most important tasks should always be first in line. Successful people make a habit of doing whatever is necessary to achieve results, even if the tasks are difficult and boring, or might stand in the way of instant gratification.

- **Standardize.** It's all right to re-invent the wheel, as long as you keep using your invention until it no longer works, or you find a way to improve it. Let's say the recruiting script you've developed gets really good results. For Pete's sake, don't change it, even if you're sick of hearing yourself recite it.

- **Economize.** Remember that not every activity or

situation requires an identical amount of effort, nor can each activity be expected to produce an identical result. For example, if a marketing call to an employer begins to disintegrate into a meaningless or unproductive gossip session, then hang up the phone and move on to the next prospect. Don't invest your time unless there's a reasonable chance of a payoff.

- **Utilize.** Whenever possible, download your tasks to other people, or tap into alternative resources or solutions. Let's say the job order you just wrote isn't worth your time recruiting for, or requires additional research that would take you away from your area of specialization. That's okay; with very little effort, you can probably get another recruiter to dig through his files, or be able to put the job order out on a network. In either case, your downloading may result in a split fee.

As a recruiter, your overarching goal is to satisfy the needs of your clients as efficiently as possible. The more quickly you work, the more satisfied you'll make the client; and ultimately, the more money you'll earn.

Sure, there's a time and place for hand-holding and time-intensive public relations efforts, but you need to make a living, not develop a *pro bono* career.

Basic Tenets of Salesmanship

The degree to which you master the art and science of selling will impact your success, since selling is intertwined with nearly every aspect of our business.

To refresh your memory, let's review some of the basic tenets of salesmanship, especially as they relate to our unique line of work:

22

- **Feature-to-benefit conversion.** Your candidate may have a Wharton MBA, sing opera and be on the fast track at Proctor & Gamble.

So what? People don't buy features, they buy the *benefits* they feel the features will give them.

For example, in order to sell more copiers, a manufacturer may stress the anti-jamming paper feeder as a feature of the machine. The subconscious selling point, of course, has nothing to do with the paper feeder; the true *benefit* of a copier that never jams is the peace of mind (or other emotional reward) that's a result of the machine's reliability. Feature-to-benefit conversion, regardless of the product or service, is the mother's milk of salesmanship.

In our business, a decision maker will intuitively gravitate towards the benefits of hiring a particular individual and overlook the candidate's features. So be on your toes, especially when marketing a candidate; the same Wharton MBA who may give one manager goose bumps may cause another to break out in a cold sweat.

Since you can't predict the precise benefits that'll arouse the interest of every decision maker you approach, you have to make an educated guess as to the most powerful benefits of any given candidate in the eyes of your market; that is, you need to select the most commonly acceptable benefit denominator and run with it.

- **Hardship identification.** This is the corollary to benefit selling, in which you remind the prospect of his greatest fears and offer a solution.

For example, when marketing your service, you could just as effectively focus on the business your client might lose without your help as you could on what the client would stand to gain as a result of your assistance. (In fact, for years recruiters have used the thinly-veiled threat, "I can either work for you or against you; it's your choice" as a means of gaining leverage.)

For maximum impact, you might try to incorporate both the benefit and loss issues into a single thought. For example, by pointing out that your candidate will enhance the performance of your client's company if he's hired but will always remain a threat while working for a direct competitor, the client stands to benefit twice --- sort of like intercepting a Joe Montana pass and returning it for a touchdown.

- **Empathy development.** There's no substitute for establishing rapport with people, and creating an environment that's conducive to selling.

Of all the rapport-building methods out there, I've found client-centered selling (CCS) to be the most effective, especially if you take the time to really learn the techniques.

In essence, client-centered selling uses empathy as a sort of machete to cut through the normal barriers that separate you and your prospect. By using non-threatening, noncommittal verbal tactics in response to concerns, CCS allows you to break down the prospect's sales resistance, thus establishing rapport, and ultimately, setting the table for a sale to occur.

Client-centered selling techniques include three basic elements:

[1] *Acknowledging*, in which you simply let the other person know you heard what they said (as in, "Uh huh, right");

[2] *Paraphrasing*, in which you rephrase the concern (as in, "Yes, Detroit *is* cold in the winter"); and

[3] *Active listening*, in which you play back the prospect's concern using a "feeling word" to show that the emotion behind the concern has been duly recorded ("You're angry at your boss for the way he treats you").

The beauty of client-centered selling is that it puts your

selling engine in idle, rather than revving it up in an attempt to hit the prospect head-on with all the logical reasons to buy, buy, buy.

There are many ways to build rapport, and every constituency will have its comfort zone, in terms of specific methodology. If you can find the technique that works best for you, you'll be way ahead of the competition (and you'll have a lot of happy customers in the process).

- **Understanding the customer's needs.** Naturally, no amount of rapport will enable you to sell the proverbial refrigerator to the Alaskan Bigfoot. Unless you can find out what the customer wants and can offer a fitting solution, you'll have little chance of making (or sustaining) a sale.

The old adage that God gave us each one mouth and two ears and that they should be used in that proportion still holds true, especially with respect to the selling profession. If you can't discipline yourself to shut up and listen to what the other side wants, you'll never reach your selling potential.

- **Qualifying.** The corollary to understanding the customer's needs, qualifying defines the selling relationship in terms of *your* needs.

In other words, if you can't reasonably expect to make a sale from the prospect, then he or she is wasting your time, at least as a buyer. (Bear in mind, though, that prospects who are unqualified to buy may exhibit extraordinary value in other areas, such as referrals).

When selling my retained search services, for example, I let my prospective customers know up front what my terms and conditions are. If they can't (or won't) ante up, then they've disqualified themselves, and I move on to another prospect.

- **Closing.** Once you've got the prospect on the hook, it's imperative to reel him in.

I have a friend who's an organizational development consultant. Not long ago, he called me with some terrific news: he had just received a signed contract from the HR director of a large corporation.

"Great," I said. "When do you start the project?"

"We're going to work that out later," he said.

"Did they say how long the project will last?"

"No," he said. "We're going to have a meeting next week to discuss the details."

"Well, I'm sure the money's good." I said.

"Actually, we never really got around to the money."

"Sounds like a great deal," I said, rolling my eyes. *Boy, he really knows how to close*, I thought.

The point is, unless you can cap off the deal, you might as well shake hands with your prospect and say, "Well, it's been nice not doing business with you."

- **Adaptability and maturity.** In order to sustain your career, it's important to see the big picture and not get discouraged by setbacks or adjustments that need to be made.

For example, I've seen many recruiters with terrific potential self-destruct by misinterpreting an objection as a deal breaker, or a delay as the bitter end.

Not every Heisman Trophy winner goes on to become the pro football rookie of the year; and likewise, not every recruiter goes on to become an instant success. It takes a lot more than mere talent to make it in this business; it takes composure, patience, flexibility and persistence.

Obviously, not every sales opportunity is going to pan out, since your desire to sell will sometimes run on a collision course with your customers' willingness to buy.

The truly great recruiters, however, recognize this fact, and continually strive to improve their odds through intelligent marketing, continuous prospecting, and the nurturing of profitable selling relationships.

Your Silent Partner at Work

While we're on the subject of selling, I'd like to stress an efficient and tireless persuasion weapon that too often tends to be overlooked: the printed word.

I like written communications because they can be used as a sort of surrogate recruiter or silent partner that works cheap, can't complain, and never gets tired.

While you're using the telephone for the urgent or highly skilled work that only you can perform (like visiting clients or closing complicated deals, for example), your silent partner can be industriously marketing your service, qualifying candidates, specifying contractual conditions, and so forth.

With your silent partner at work, you can still make as many phone calls as you need; you'll just be eliminating a lot of wasted time and effort.

Make no mistake; written communications are no substitute for the skills recruiters need to master in order to succeed. A direct mail letter, for example, can't calm the nerves of a candidate's spouse who's facing a relocation to Guadalajara, or instill a foot-dragging hiring manager with a sense of urgency. But in many incremental (and not-so-incremental) ways, what you write can favorably influence the people you do business with.

A Myriad of Powerful Tools

When you associate the printed word with our particular business, documents such as resumes, fee schedules and miscellaneous promotional materials usually come to mind.

However, these represent the mere tip of the iceberg. Written communications can also include powerful, time-saving tools such as custom cover letters, proposals, contracts, direct mail letters, navigators, search logs, interview preparation guides, position comparisons, reference checks, customer surveys, and a wide range of other instruments

27

designed to enhance your efficiency and increase your billings.

The same boss of mine who believed in the monkey at the typewriter theory also thought it was a waste of time to write letters to clients. "No one reads anything anymore," he used to say.

He's right, of course --- if you write the wrong letter to the wrong person at the wrong time. However, by adding carefully crafted letters and a myriad of effective written communications to your business vocabulary, you'll increase your overall commercial impact, and free up a lot of your time in the process.

**By using all the selling tools available,
you'll quickly increase your income.**

2

Market Your Service with Power and Efficiency

Marketing is one of the least understood aspects of the recruiting business. More time is spent obsessing over marketing than any other activity; yet ironically, more time, energy and money is wasted through ineffective marketing than any other activity.

First, let's clear the air and define the term. Marketing is simply *the planning or infrastructure that causes a sale to be made.* Or, put another way, marketing is like the software that allows you to work productively on your computer. Without the requisite planning that marketing provides, a buyer and seller will drift like two ships in the night, with any sales activity occurring more by accident than by design.

Developing a Comprehensive Marketing Strategy

Many recruiters skim the surface of marketing without ever burrowing deeply into its essential elements. For example, making a hundred cold calls may be *related* to marketing, but smiling and dialing by itself can hardly be considered a comprehensive strategy.

To develop a marketing infrastructure, six key issues must be addressed: who, what, where, when, why and how.

Only after you've quantified the essential elements of your market can you begin to put together a workable plan that directly attacks the market, and exploits its full potential.

[1] Who is your target market?

This is the most basic consideration in your planning. As you probably know, markets are usually defined in terms of *vertical* versus *horizontal*. In the employment world, that roughly translates to industry versus skill (or position title).

In a vertical market such as plastics, your universe would include any number of skill sets or titles within that particular industry. Naturally, you have the freedom to choose the depth and specificity of your constituency. In the plastics world, you may decide to fill positions like engineering and sales, but not HR, data processing, clerical, or general management.

Likewise, in a horizontal (or skill based) market such as the legal profession, you may also focus your search activities. For example, you may concentrate on commercial law or litigation, but stay away from environmental, criminal or regulatory law.

Regardless of your vertical or horizontal orientation, you may further define your niche by targeting a certain salary bracket, organizational size, geographic location, product specialty (web, not offset printing, for example), decision-maker customer base (HR versus president versus MIS manager), and so forth.

A terrific way to seek out or define the boundaries of a target market is to identify with an existing trade or professional association.

Believe it or not, there are over 22,000 such societies listed in the *Encyclopedia of Associations,* a book that can be found in your local library. These homogeneous interest groups include everything from the generic (the American Business Women's Association) to the specific (the Association of Industrial Lighting Distributors) to the esoteric (the Society of Biological Psychiatry).

Once you get your hands on a group's directory, buyer's guide or trade magazine, you'll be able to quickly identify a potential target population; and by joining the group, you'll gain access to its membership, boost your professional credibility, and earn "insider" status.

[2] What is the nature of your service?

Are you a specialist or a generalist? Contingency or retainer? Flat fee or sliding fee? High level or low level constituency? Local, national or international? Headhunter or full-service human resource consultant? Placer of candidates or filler of positions?

The more tightly you can define your service (and the image you project), the better you'll be able to position yourself in the market.

One of the most useful things you can do to clarify your position in the market is to perform a *competitive analysis.* Find out who you're up against, and see how they work, how they position themselves, what type of image they project, their pricing structure, and what their customers feel they do right and wrong.

Since it's very difficult to work in a vacuum, survey your customers from time to time, and ask them what functional or public relations improvements would benefit your business from their perspective.

[3] When are your customers in a position to buy?

Selling cycles are an important consideration in your marketing infrastructure, since they affect not only your cash flow but your desk psychology.

Generally speaking, the lower the position level, the faster the placement process; the higher the level, the longer the wait.

If you jump from placing programmers to presidents, you'd better be able to weather the ebb and flow of a six month, rather than a six week incubation period.

Organizational size also has a lot to do with each customer's buying potential. It goes without saying that a company must have the financial resources to pay a fee and/or be able to provide you with repeat business. Otherwise, you may find yourself in a constant collection mode, or scattered across a client base consisting of a dozen little companies unable to afford your services after the first placement has been made.

[4] How do you reach your target market?

The delivery system you use to disseminate your message will vary, according to the five other elements. In your particular constituency, with your particular service, will telephone cold calling be the most effective approach? Or will face-to-face meetings (or letters, or display advertising or soft-sell PR materials) produce the best results?

Experienced marketers constantly tweak their message delivery systems and experiment with methods that will hopefully bring a better return on their investment. No improvement is too small; for example, I make slight corrections in my marketing communications materials nearly once a month. Cumulatively, the effect has been dramatic.

[5] Why would anyone want to buy from you?

Business differentiation (or at the very least, the buyer's

perception that you're different) is critical in a free market.

Ask yourself: What can you do for the customer that they can't do for themselves or can't get from your competition?

Think about it: Are you distinguished by your industry connections, your fast turnaround, your ability to understand needs, your rapport with managers, your business ethics, or some other tangible or intangible characteristic that puts you head and shoulders above the rest of the crowd?

If you can't pinpoint your business differentiation, then it's likely your customers can't either, and you need to spend some time on your business plan, reviewing your fundamental *raison d'être*.

[6] Where are the needs within your target market?

You may have the best price, best service, best promotional literature and loftiest ethics of any recruiter on the planet, but if you're trying to fill a need that doesn't exist, you're going to find it awful tough to make a living.

The question of "need" in the recruiting business has reached critical mass in the post-recessionary shakeout, given the large number of companies downsizing, outsourcing or utilizing new technologies.

To test for employment needs in a given industry, there are several yardsticks you can use. These include:

- **Financial health.** Are the companies in your field going boom or bust?

- **Growth.** Are new businesses in your field starting up, or are entrepreneurs avoiding your industry like the plague?

- **Government contracts.** Are state, local and federal monies being spent to develop your industry, in the form of purchases, new construction or research grants?

- **Government regulations.** Are new laws (such as environmental controls, safety requirements, tax restructuring or import tariffs) positively or negatively affecting the employment needs of your industry?

- **Litigation.** Are recent court rulings (and their commercial ramifications) having an affect on your industry?

- **Demographics.** Are certain geographic areas ramping up in terms of desirability or population growth? If the answer is yes, and you happen to specialize in the hospitality or retail industries, then new vacation and retirement hot spots would be of particular interest.

- **New technologies.** Are the advances in product design, science, manufacturing, workplace automation and the art of management placing demands on modern employers? If so, there will certainly be needs to be filled.

It would be an understatement to say that the ability to find and fill needs is fundamental to success, whether you're selling a recruiting service, a luxury car or a pet rock. If you don't know where the needs are, then unfortunately, there's no way to satisfy them.

Spotting Trends or Chasing Rainbows?

While it's important to monitor demographic and economic trends (who, for example, would consciously get into aerospace recruiting these days?), recruiting is a very "nichey" business. Believe me, I'd be the last person to know where the "hot" industries are; I'm too busy making money within my own constituency to come up for air. As far as I'm concerned, the expression "all politics is local" generally applies to recruiting as well as government.

Market misidentification has been the downfall of many recruiters who have either lusted after glitzy industries like biotech, or have fiddled with dying smokestack industries while Rome burned around them. My heart really goes out to recruiters who've pinned their hopes on "hot" niches that turned out to be a flash in the pan; or to those who've picked through the mother lodes that have already been mined to death.

Expanding Your Market for Higher Billings

I know it sounds a bit trite, but the expression, "the only thing that stays the same is change" is a business truism, especially in the employment game. Inevitably, your market will change, your customers will change, and you'll change, too. As sales trainer Brian Tracy once said, everyone wants things to stay the same, only get better. The problem is, unless you win the lottery, life doesn't work that way.

The best way to deal with change is not to ignore it, but to counter (or exploit) its effects through growth and experimentation.

Here's what I mean: Unless you have a crystal ball, it's impossible to guess exactly what's coming down the pike. You might guess right, but then again, you may not, and a wrong guess may have disastrous consequences.

However, if you're constantly seeking different ways to develop your existing market to its fullest (that is, increase your market share), and to expand your reach into peripheral markets, you'll hedge your bets against the inevitable decline of particular industries, sponsors or employment markets. Or better yet, through the process of growth and experimentation, you may just stumble upon an emerging commercial trend that will pay dividends for years to come.

It's sort of like investing. If you've ever tried to make your assets grow, you'll know from experience that the most cautious (and some might say, the most wise) approach is to maintain a balanced portfolio that contains CDs, mutual funds, stocks, treasury bills and so forth.

In our business, the strategy for growth plays itself out like this:

[1]   *Go deep.* That is, expand the range of salary levels and position titles within your constituency. For example, when I was faced with a declining engineering market, I bumped my business into sales, marketing and general management --- but within the industry I already knew and had credibility in.

[2]   *Go broad.* In other words, expand the range of related businesses or SIC codes you market to. Not long ago, I found that there was a lot of business in high tech construction and utility products. While neither the construction nor the utility markets were ever part of my constituency, I found that they were close fitting enough with my existing market to benefit from my expertise, and provide me with income.

[3]   *Go boldly.* Try approaches to your business (such as marketing, pricing, policy or scope) that have a fighting chance for success. You may surprise yourself and actually excel in some area that you previously ignored or were afraid to try. I've known contingency recruiters who've hit it big with retained work (and vice versa), temp agencies that added permanent placement to their list of services (and vice versa), and pen and pencil outfits that went *cyberspace* (via the Internet).

A few years ago, when I started my own search practice, I spent several sessions with a gentleman named Chuck

Weideman, who was my "mentor" through the Small Business Administration's Service Corps of Retired Executives (SCORE) program.

Chuck's 50-year career was spent as an international business consultant; and he often told me that the motto that appeared atop his firm's stationery should have read "Anything for a buck."

It was Chuck who constantly chided me for being too conservative and afraid to try new things. After a while, I guess Chuck's advice sunk in, and I started sending up trial balloons, some of which popped, and some of which developed into full blown and significant income streams.

Defining Your Service and Carving Out a Niche

During the depths of the last economic recession, it became clear that the fat and happy days of recruiting were over, at least for the foreseeable future.

To buck the downward trend in my own business, I developed a strategy designed to clarify my role in the employment market, since my freewheeling, all-things-to-all-people approach was no longer working. In so doing, I repositioned myself in the market as a high-end, highly structured specialist in executive search and human resource consulting.

To this end, I began to offer various types of clearly delineated services to my clients, rather than try to compete in the crowded *mosh pit* of contingency search.

This was a tactical, not a judgmental decision. I was faced with the fact that at the time, there were simply too many hungry people out there with too little pie to go around. For every open position I was trying to fill, there were at least three other recruiters with the same job order, sending in candidates of more or less equal ability (sure, I'm good at finding high quality candidates, but so was my competition).

To fight back, I borrowed a page right out of the classic

marketing textbook --- I took an equivalent product and repackaged it to appeal to a different set of buyers. By so doing, I was able to reposition my service and distance myself from the competition.

A Choice, Not an Echo

To start with, I began to offer my clients a choice of search *programs*, depending on the salary level of the position they wanted to fill.

The Radin Associates *exclusive retained executive search* program, for example, pertains to positions with starting salaries greater than $100,000; while the *modified retained search* program offers roughly the same service, but for positions between $50,000 and $100,000.

Out of strategic necessity, I stopped recruiting for positions paying less than $50,000 a year. There were two reasons for this. First, because of the relatively low fees, they weren't worth my time; and second, these types of positions were just too hard to fill.

Here's what I mean. In my area of specialization, the competitive high tech world, I've found that candidates making below $50,000 usually lack the "career mentality" that drives them to improve their professional standing.

Because their careers take a back seat to other facets of their lives (which is fine, I'm not making a value judgment), these types of candidates are less hungry to take the risks or make the sacrifices that are part and parcel with upward mobility.

Usually, the flash point with *refusenik* candidates is relocation, which is a non-negotiable fact of life in niche market advancement. In my experience, it's a waste of energy to try to persuade career-stagnant candidates to relocate, just like it's a waste of time to beat on a mule to make the animal kick into gear.

I made the choice to exclude a certain segment of the employment market as a way to reposition my service, and the strategy paid off. Would the same strategy work for you? I guess that depends on who you are and where you want to go, and how badly you want to get there.

All I know is that there's money to be made by providing service to every color in the economic spectrum; where you look for the pot of gold is entirely up to you.

Method Behind the Madness

The *program* approach to recruiting deals with more than just pricing and positioning; it also deals with the exact nature of the search methodology and the way the services are explained to the client.

When we discuss the process of executing a search, I tell my clients that there are three phases involved:

[1]   *Recruit.* We begin by identifying individuals who possess the technical and motivational qualifications that the client defines; and after careful screening, we schedule face-to-face interviews with the most highly qualified candidates.

[2]   *Offer.* After sincere and mutual interest is determined, we assist in negotiating an acceptable compensation package with the finalist.

[3]   *Transition.* Once the offer is formally accepted, we help provide for a smooth physical relocation and incorporation into the client's company, both by counseling the new hire on proper resignation procedures and by helping facilitate the move.

This three-phase explanation works like a charm, in that it helps sell the client on my service, exposes any objections or misunderstandings he may have, and precloses the client on our mutual responsibilities.

Secondary Streams of Income

To add value to the service I provide, I also offer my clients an assortment of side dishes relating to the client's current (and ever changing) staffing and human resource needs. These include:

- **Candidate screening.** Some clients are good at generating candidate flow, but lack the expertise or manpower to adequately separate the wheat from the chaff. By outsourcing the selection process to me, they can save themselves time, money and aggravation.

- **Competitive analysis.** On a project basis, I'll be happy to root around my client's competitors and develop an organizational chart, or put together a list of key contributors.

- **Spot recruiting.** When the client has a particular individual in mind that they would like to recruit, I can assume the role of a discreet third party to make the initial overture. In these cases, I charge an hourly fee, which is credited against the search fee if the individual ultimately joins my client's organization.

- **Market research.** Sales directors are very curious about their companies' reputation for quality, service, delivery, responsiveness and so forth. To help them out, I'll conduct a telephone survey with the clients' customers.

- **Reference checking.** Some clients lack the internal know-how or objectivity to assess the merits of candidates. When such a situation arises, I can contact the references for them, and write a detailed report.

- **Outsourcing referrals.** Executive recruiters only fill permanent positions --- Not! We also refer consultants, contractors and third-party sales channels such as manufacturers' reps, distributors, systems integrators and value-added resellers (VARs).

- **Psychometric testing.** If a candidate's personality or aptitude for the job are in question (and the client has no staff psychologist), I'll arrange for testing through a licensed industrial psychologist or organizational development professional.

These services can be billed on a fixed, cost-plus or hourly rate, depending on their scope and level of difficulty or expertise required. (For hourly services, you can charge anywhere from $50 to $200 per hour, plus expenses). Even though your core business may be recruiting, why turn up your nose at these nifty little streams of income?

More Choices Mean More Value

One search firm I know will accept search assignments for sales people only if the client companies they work with agree to let the search firm provide sales training for all their new hires.

The rationale for this value-added service goes like this: Since the search firm has an expertise in sales, their training will not only enhance the new hires' skills (and in turn, the client companies' profits), but will ensure the longevity of the new hires, thus saving the clients from paying additional search fees in the future. A great idea, guys.

I'm not suggesting you drop everything you're doing in order to sell these types of services; doing so would be analogous to owning a restaurant and dropping all the entrees

41

from your menu in order to offer only appetizers.

But as any successful restaurateur will tell you, there's lots of money (and customer satisfaction) to be gained from offering an attractive selection of pleasing side dishes.

Finding a Parade to Lead

Though it's totally devoid of glamour, the trial and error approach to finding the new business within your market is often the most effective method. If you're already keyed in to the critical employment needs of your industry, great. If not, shift (or expand) your focus to another segment of your constituency, or look for another industry to serve.

Don't spend an inordinate amount of time overanalyzing data or trying to second guess your situation. Sure, you can sift through mountains of government surveys that index the employment forecasts of the next decade --- as long as you bear in mind that statistics such as the "BLS moderate growth scenarios for non-farm manufacturing employment" may produce more of a headache than a business prophesy.

Even if you do manage to latch onto a "hot" industry, you need to take into account the fact that an employer's hiring needs will be tempered with his or her ability to pay a fee.

For example, the fast food industry represents a growing employment sector of our economy. And on any given Sunday, there are 500 openings listed in the help wanted ads. But does that mean that the manager at the local Burger King will pay you a fee to find a night shift condiment supervisor?

The specific amount of time and energy you invest in new market development is a very personal matter, since we each have a different return-on-investment threshold. However, if you find yourself spending six months and getting very little in the way of results, it may be time to look into other areas of specialization.

Remember, the trick to establishing a successful market niche is to find a suitable parade, walk in front of it --- and get someone to pay you for it.

Market Forces Will Necessitate Change

Rarely can anyone in our field be forever insulated from the various demographic forces controlling the employment market. In my own practice, for example, I found that the "rank and file" engineers that were in such high demand in the 1980s drew barely a yawn from employers by the early 1990s. In other words, the specialized population that was once my bread and butter had become a mere commodity.

In order to survive, I had to alter my constituency; and since everything in this business is interdependent, I had to fine tune my approach to marketing to adjust to the change.

If you're lucky enough to be carried smoothly over the bumps in the recruiting road by a wave of sheer momentum, hats off to you. For most of us, though, our success will rest in our ability to adapt to change, in our steady application of common sense, and in the fundamental skills we possess as street-smart sales professionals.

**By implementing a sound marketing
strategy, your business is certain to thrive.**

Fig. 2.1 Clearly defined services will distinguish you from the competition.

Radin Associates
Executive Search Programs

Under our retained search programs, Radin Associates will be given, by agreement, exclusive rights for recruiting, interviewing, screening, and selecting finalists for specific positions. These finalists are then interviewed by the client.

An effective and successful search begins by meeting with those corporate officials most impacted by the hiring of a specific candidate. The objective is to accurately define the position responsibilities, reporting relationships, short-term and long-term goals, and expected interactions with staff, management, customers, and providers of external services. In addition to defining the candidate's required technical and educational credentials, we will construct a profile (or *navigator*) that describes a qualified candidate in terms of temperament, work habits, career drive, and personal bearing. A position outline will be drawn up that details the mandatory/preferred qualifications covering past and current employment history, years of specific experience, and salary and relocation parameters.

Exclusive Retained Executive Search (Starting salary at $100,000 or above)
• *Search Fee:* The fee for our service is calculated at one-third (33.3%) of the hired candidate's estimated first year compensation.
• *Payment:* An advanced retainer of one-third of the estimated search fee is due Radin Associates upon acceptance of the assignment. One-third of the search fee is due 30 days after acceptance, with the final one-third of the search fee due 60 days after acceptance.
• *Expenses:* All approved telephone, facsimile, overnight delivery, and travel expenses directly related to the assignment are billed separately.
• *Guarantee:* If the placed candidate terminates or is terminated from his or her position for any reason other than lack of work within sixty (60) days of his or her date of start, Radin Associates will find a suitable replacement within a reasonable period of time following the termination.

Modified Retained Search (Starting salary between $50,000 and $100,000)
• *Search Fee:* The fee for our service is calculated at one-third (33.3%) of the hired candidate's estimated first year compensation.
• *Payment:* An advanced retainer of one-third of the estimated search fee is due Radin Associates upon acceptance of the assignment. The balance of the search fee is due upon start date of the referred candidate.
• *Expenses:* All approved telephone, facsimile, overnight delivery, and travel expenses directly related to the assignment are billed separately.
• *Guarantee:* If the placed candidate terminates or is terminated from his or her position for any reason other than lack of work within sixty (60) days of his or her date of start, Radin Associates will find a suitable replacement within a reasonable period of time following the termination.

3

Exploit
Your Market's
Full
Potential

Now that we've examined various ways to identify a base of potential customers, the next step is to find the proper methods by which we can get our message across to them.

A marketing campaign is very much like a political campaign. In order to win, you have to "connect" with as many voters (or, in our case, prospective clients) as possible, by whatever means are available.

Just as television is the medium of choice with politicians, the telephone is the principal instrument of recruiters.

Cold calling by telephone has and will continue to be the centerpiece of our business, in terms of direct marketing technique. Cold calling allows you to make contact with real prospects and generate interest in your service. The meaningful dialogue you create not only allows you to understand the prospect's needs, it also provides you with the means to "bond," or build rapport with the person on the other end of the line.

The Perils and Profits of Picking Up the Phone

Cold calling works --- as long as certain conditions are met. Otherwise, your cold calling efforts could be frustrating, nonproductive, or even counterproductive.

[1] You must contact qualified prospects;

[2] You must offer your prospects something that they need and can afford; and

[3] You must be able to verbally articulate your ability to fill the prospects' needs in a coherent and professional manner.

Once you satisfy these criteria, cold calling can work beautifully, since telephone prospecting is the most expedient and direct way to make contact with prospective customers. When a telephone conversation is properly executed, the information you gather is far more revealing and objective than if you met the prospect face to face, or made contact by a letter or fax transmission.

Negating the Schwarzenegger Effect

I'm convinced the human voice has its own "body language." That is, if you listen really closely to the person you're speaking with, you'll find that emotions such as guilt, fear, indecision, anger and elation can really leap out of the telephone at you. The better you're able to decipher these types of encoded messages, the more they can help you build selling relationships.

Vocal body language interpretation can also spare you a lot of grief. For example, if a person's going to fudge the truth, I'd prefer he or she do it over the phone, where I can really zero in on their vocal quality. In a face-to-face meeting, the person's physical appearance or the surroundings are likely to cause distractions.

To me, the phone is the perfect place to get down to business, since you and the other party are always on equal footing. The words you exchange cut right to the chase, without regard to who has the Rolex watch, the Armani suit or the Schwarzenegger physique.

Seven Keys to Telephone Prospecting

Assuming your service is marketable, and you've created a workable list of viable prospects, a cold calling campaign must contain these seven key elements in order to be most effective:

[1] *Regularity.* As any body builder will tell you, it does a lot more good to lift a 10-pound weight 20 times a week than it does to lift a 200-pound weight once a week. Not only should you keep to a regular schedule of prospecting, you should make sure to repeat your calls to each prospect several times a quarter. That way, you'll establish your name recognition, professional credibility and interest in doing business over the long haul.

[2] *Consistency of message.* As time goes by, your customer base will get to know you; and the more often you repeat the benefits of your service and the way you differentiate yourself from the competition, the more likely you'll be to link up with a prospect, and land an account.

47

[3] *Sincerity of delivery.* There's a certain "drama" to cold calling. Just like when you're giving a speech, you must sell your audience on your belief in what you're saying. If you come across as bored, tired, insincere, or lacking in the belief that what you're offering is worth ten times the price you're asking, then you might as well hang up the phone.

[4] *Multitasking.* By setting clear and specific goals surrounding your telephone prospecting activities, you'll be able to accomplish a great deal from each call. For example, the main purpose of a particular call may be to write a job order. However, if you fail, there's no reason you can't succeed in several other areas, such as gathering company information, general industry data, profile information on the person you're calling, present and future job order leads at the prospect's company or at other companies, and so forth. Multitasking your calls in this manner can really pay off; it's like getting 100 miles on a single gallon of gas.

[5] *Dialogue creation.* The more you engage your prospect in dialogue, the more likely you'll build trust, and break down the barriers separating you and the prospect from doing business together.

[6] *Rapport building.* Once you've established your ability to converse, you must make it clear that you can relate to your prospect's interests, and can empathize with whatever his or her staffing needs may be. In a trust-based business such as ours, rapport will inevitably lead to sales activity, either directly or indirectly.

[7] *Follow-up.* Whenever you promise to do something

for a client, make sure to honor your commitment, whether it's sending a letter, paying a visit, or making a return phone call at a specified time. Unfortunately, in today's society, relationships have become disposable and personal responsibility a mere vestige of the past. By demonstrating your trustworthiness, you'll earn the right to do business with your prospects (and get yourself put on the "A" list for future assignments).

Cold calling is an imprecise science in that you can never predict the ultimate outcome of each call. However, by building rapport, asking the right questions and keeping your ears open, there's a good possibility that every call you make will pay off in some way or another.

The Power of Active Calls

In my experience, the most effective type of cold call is an *active* call, one in which you present the prospect with an idea that calls for a decision. Here are some tried and true variations:

- **MPA (or most placeable applicant) calls.** By presenting a potentially valuable candidate to a prospective employer, you can create meaningful dialogue, probe for needs, gather industry information, and, if the moons and planets are properly aligned, set the stage for a placement by arranging a sendout. At the very least, a well-executed MPA call will enable you to build credibility with the prospect and associate your services with high-quality and appropriate industry talent, and establish your professional identity.

- **Indirect recruiting calls.** In many ways, search assignments can create excellent marketing opportunities. For example, by asking a top-level manager for help in identifying outstanding candidates, you'll position yourself as an industry expert, poised and ready to help the manager with any of his or her critical staffing needs.

- **Professional reference calls.** Your thoroughness and commitment to helping your clients are qualities certain to make a positive impression on hiring managers. Therefore, it only makes sense to offer your services at the completion of a telephone reference check.

- **Staffing center calls.** The next time you schedule an EIO (employer in office), you can call the hiring managers at other companies who might benefit from interviewing your candidates. If all goes well, your EIO will attract several employers, each of whom will be vying for the same group of candidates. (For a complete description of EIO techniques, please see chapter 9.)

Active calls are great because they give you and the prospect something to talk about. In contrast, I've found that service calls, or *passive* calls are okay, but generally lack the immediate impact that characterizes telephone prospecting.

If the main purpose for launching a marketing campaign is to achieve name recognition or sow the seeds of future client development, then other approaches such as display advertising or direct mail marketing could be more time- and cost-effective.

The Importance of Scripts

Consciously or otherwise, each of us uses word patterns in

our everyday business dealings. And the more deliberate and thoughtful the phraseology we use, the more we're able to accomplish.

When word patterns are crafted in such a way as to set the agenda or steer the conversation towards a certain outcome, we call them scripts.

Mostly, we think of scripts as tools that can be used during activities such as telephone prospecting, either to spark initial interest in a candidate, expose a prospect's concern, or refute a misconception.

However, scripting can also be invaluable in a variety of other situations, such as recruiting, closing, and in preparing yourself for important conversations, in which there are a number of specific points that need to be covered. By scripting the sequence and "spin" you want to put on each talking point, you'll save yourself time and future aggravation.

Common Denominators
Produce Tangible Results

Scripts designed specifically for marketing are endless in their variety; however, all scripts should have certain features in common. These include:

- **A strong opening line.** Also known as a *hook* or *grabber*, your script should contain an opening statement or series of sentences that grabs and holds the attention of the prospect.

- **An open-ended question.** This should immediately follow your opening line. A strong open-ended question is designed to test the acceptance of your grabber, and create dialogue. At this point in the conversation, it's unlikely you'll be in a position to "close" on anything; rather, what you want to do is give the prospect the opportunity to freely discuss his or her needs or concerns.

- **Acknowledging the information you receive.** People hate to feel like they're being hustled. By letting the prospect know that you heard what he said (in a neutral manner, without putting pressure on him), you'll not only build rapport, you'll be in a better position to understand, and eventually fill, his needs. If you think of the telemarketing calls you receive at home, I'm sure you'll agree that the most annoying characteristic is the total lack of interest the salesperson shows for your unique needs. The ability to listen is what distinguishes a good recruiter from a run-of-the-mill telemarketer.

- **Initiate a trial close.** Assuming the prospect's needs coincide with what you have to offer, the time is probably right to receive a commitment from the prospect, either in the form of a sendout, a marketing appointment, a search assignment, a proposal, a referral, a call back at a later time, or any other result you've set as a cold calling goal.

In other words, each cold call should produce a tangible result, even if the result is "they won't be in a position to hire until March," or, "that prospect sure is difficult to deal with. The next time I call, I'll take a different approach."

Make sure you keep a file on every prospect you've spoken to, and what was accomplished during the conversation. That way, the next time you call, your script will already be written; you can simply build on the previous conversation.

These Are a Few of My Favorite Scripts

The cold calls I make are generally targeted at senior level executives. Therefore, I try to adjust my scripts to match their particular syntax and business rhythms.

Because your constituency might differ from mine, I can't promise you that what works for me will work for you, but the general principles will still apply.

That being said, here are a few of my favorite scripts. The first one is an MPA presentation.

Recruiter: *Mr. Employer, my name is Bill Radin, and I'm calling from Santa Fe, New Mexico. Have I caught you at a bad time?*

Employer: *No time is a good time, but go ahead.*

Recruiter: *Okay. This is not very complicated, but it does need a bit of explanation.*

I'm the president of a very highly specialized executive search firm. For the past ten years, I've worked exclusively in the sensor industry, concentrating on people who have talent in the sales and marketing arena.

The reason I wanted to get in touch with you is that because of my visibility in this very niche market, I've been approached by an individual who's got a long list of accomplishments in the industry. In fact, right now he's what you might call a "high-impact player" with a direct competitor of yours, but has always admired your company, and felt he could do great things for you if only the opportunity were there.

He's asked me to inquire, discreetly, whether or not you might have an interest in talking with him, to see if he could do for you some of the truly outstanding things he's done with his present company.

Do you think you might be receptive to this idea?

Even if the employer lacks an interest in this particular candidate, you can bet he's going to remember the fact that I specialize in his industry, and represent quality individuals.

The next marketing script directly follows a recruiting call, in which the employer has just referred a past employee.

Recruiter: *Mr. Employer, I can't thank you enough for passing along Pat's name. I think you're right; he'd be ideal for the position.*

But before I let you go, I can't help but ask you: Are there any critical staffing needs at your company right now?

Employer: *Well, there are, but to tell you the truth, we're very reluctant to use a recruiter.*

Recruiter: *That makes sense. I know I'd rather have a root canal than pay good money to an accountant to do my taxes. The only problem is, I'd be in jail right now if it weren't for him.*

Employer: *Well, I guess we can keep you in mind, if we really get stuck.*

Recruiter: *Tell you what. If you've got just a minute, I'd like to learn more about what sort of person you're looking for. If by some miracle I happen to know someone who fits the bill, then maybe I can save you a lot of time and aggravation. If not, as they say, no harm, no foul.*

Employer: *Well, I guess it couldn't hurt to clue you in.*

Recruiter: *Great. Let me a get out a piece of paper, and I'll take a few notes.*

What I really want to do in this situation is get a feel for the type of person the manager would find valuable to the organization, and start building a selling relationship with him.

Sure, I might make a placement. But more importantly, by allowing the employer to open up to me, I'm setting the stage for future client development.

The Staffing Center Script

The last script is one that I've used in a contingency search situation, where I want to maximize my chances of making a placement.

Recruiter: *Mr. Employer, I appreciate your taking my call. I wondered if you could help me.*

Employer: *Look, I'm on my way out the door to catch a flight to Pittsburgh. Can it wait until next week?*

Recruiter: *I'll tell you what. Let me cover the salient points in the next 30 seconds, and if what we talk about requires more time next week, let's schedule a time when we can get together.*

Employer: *Okay, you've got 30 seconds. Go.*

Recruiter: *All right. First let me tell you who I am. I'm a high-level executive recruiter, and I specialize in the instrumentation field. Over the past ten years, I've filled several key positions for companies that are well known in the industry.*

Next Thursday, I've got a staffing center scheduled for one of my clients, a company that manufactures products that are compatible, not competitive with yours.

At the staffing center will be a number of extremely talented candidates who've each worked in your industry for a number of years, and have made tremendous contributions.

I know it's unlikely that you might have an

interest in upgrading your staff at this particular time; however, I felt it would be in everyone's best interest if your company were included in the session, just in case you felt a first-round draft choice might help your team.

What would be the likelihood of your wanting to attend?

As in an MPA presentation, I want to position myself as an industry expert who has the ability to attract premium quality candidates on short notice.

A "staffing center," by the way, is the way I refer to an EIO to those outside the recruiting industry.

By following the fundamental principles of telephone cold calling, you can increase your efficiency, regardless of your constituency, or the precise syntax your script employs.

Alternative Marketing Techniques

Just as the savvy politician might employ methods other than TV advertising to reach all possible voters (such as billboard ads or door-to-door soliciting), the savvy recruiter can expand his or her business by using alternative techniques in addition to telephone cold calling.

To balance your marketing efforts, here are several ways to get your message across to prospective clients:

- **Generic group marketing.** If the prospect pool is appropriate, you can give a speech to your local Chamber of Commerce or Kiwanis Club. With a benefit-oriented speech title like "How to boost productivity in the work force," or, "How to attract the highest quality employees," you're sure to attract an audience, and position yourself for new business development.

- **Generic mingle marketing.** Local business

organizations such as the Chamber sponsor breakfast, lunch and dinner meetings at which you can "network" with other members.

- **Industry-specific group marketing.** To deepen your penetration, give the same speech you practiced on the Kiwanis to your target market at your industry's next association meeting.

- **Industry-specific mingle marketing.** At the same association meeting or convention, mingle amongst the membership in the exhibit hall or at the awards banquet. With any luck, you'll make a positive impression on prospective clients.

- **Display advertising.** If you have the budget to do so, consider running a display ad or classified ad in your industry's newsletter or trade magazine; or, if your target market is local, in your town's business weekly or Chamber publication. Although the respondents to such ads will consist mostly of job-seekers, you'll increase your overall visibility with employers looking to fill positions.

- **Article insertion.** In your industry's newsletter or trade magazine, write an article similar to the speech you gave at the last convention. The interest you generate will in all likelihood spawn a job order or two; or at the very least, the resulting name recognition will help position you as an industry authority.

- **"Outside" sales.** Whenever I visit a client company, I pay close attention to the physical surroundings. If the client's office is in an industrial park or office complex (and I'm in a what-the-heck mood), I'll pay an unannounced visit to similar businesses and ask the receptionist if I may speak to the engineering manager or operations director. With a little luck, I'll get the chance to chat with a prospective customer, or at the very least, drop off a business card or two.

- **Direct mail marketing.** Even with the rise in postage costs, direct mail represents one of the most cost-effective methods of reaching a large number of potential prospects. (For a complete description of direct mail marketing techniques, see chapter 13.)

While you or I may never attain (or seek) name recognition with the general public, we certainly should strive to become "famous" among those in our target market. The more often your customers associate your name with quality staffing results, the more often you'll make placements.

**To grow your business,
exploit your market's full potential
by every means possible.**

4

Increase the Level of Client Commitment

The degree of any client's commitment can be measured very simply: by the quality of the job orders he or she gives you.

As you already know, many of the job orders you write will turn out to be bogus; and sadly, the time and energy you spend trying to fill these black hole orders could more productively be spent on other activities, such as referring candidates for cooperative, qualified employers who have genuine needs.

If you take a look at how and why your job orders turn to dust, you'll probably recognize a few of the ways that your clients let you down:

- **False sense of urgency.** The employer isn't actually positioned to hire anyone at this time (or in the foreseeable future, for that matter), regardless of how well your candidates fit the position specifications.

- **Unrealistic expectations.** The "ideal" candidate doesn't exist, can't be found, or can't be attracted to the employer's organization.

- **Drifting search parameters.** The employer's grand vision of the perfect candidate's qualifications, job responsibilities and interview-to-offer timeline wanders like Moses in the Sinai.

- **Hidden agenda.** The employer's search is wired. That is, the hiring manager has already chosen a candidate and is simply manipulating you to justify or validate a *fait accompli* within the organization.

Of course, job order meltdown is a two-way street. Like it or not, we each have to assume responsibility for orders that go unfilled or are lost to our competitors.

Two Can Play the Blame Game

When it comes to job orders that fizzle, there's usually plenty of blame to go around. Here's how recruiters have been known to drop the ball:

- **Sloppy qualifying.** We incorrectly assume that the company we're dealing with is sincere and precisely focused on who they want to hire.

- **Tunnel vision.** We lead ourselves to believe that the employer's position is attractive to recruited candidates; or that we have a leg up on the competition, even though we may be outnumbered.

- **Insufficient information gathering.** We get lazy and fail to sufficiently understand the position, the company's needs, the selling points of the opportunity, and so on. The result? Wasted recruiting time, presentation of poorly matched candidates, and loss of credibility with the client.

- **Excessive pride or misplaced sympathy.** We take on the "impossible" search, only to find that there aren't a lot of seven-foot tall entry-level Harvard MBAs with red hair willing to relocate to Albuquerque to work for a fertilizer company.

- **Inability to perform.** We lack the resources to get the job done; we're either too busy working on something else, or we try to fill a position outside our area of expertise.

- **Reluctance to establish authority.** We allow the employer to set the ground rules for the search, leaving us in a perpetual posture of weakness.

If any of these miscues sound familiar, welcome to the club. The question is, how do we establish control of our job order activity?

The Doormat Approach to Executive Recruiting

For years, I wrote job orders in the traditional way: I filled out a J.O. form over the telephone, and if I had the courage, sent a fee schedule to the employer. The whole process took maybe 45 minutes.

In retrospect, it's hard to believe how carelessly I depleted my time resources. Often, with nothing more than a phone call and a few scribbled notes as backup, I would spend 20 or 30 hours chasing down candidates I hoped might be acceptable to the client. Talk about a leap of faith!

Well, it's all part of the numbers game, I told myself. *Some of these turkeys will fly, and some will drop like a lead balloon.*

This sort of rationalization works if you have an inexhaustible tolerance to act as a doormat for insincere or unqualified customers. It took a lot of time, but for me, this approach finally got old.

That Burning Sensation

The last straw was a contingency search I did for a multinational corporation looking for a president for one of its divisions. The fee would have been in the neighborhood of $35,000, so I was motivated; however, the clincher for this "hot" job order was the assurance of exclusivity given to me by the corporate HR director.

In retrospect, the only thing I did right was get the client to agree to pay my telephone expenses.

You guessed it; I got reamed. Not only did the employer stretch the interviewing process out to three months, jerk my candidates around and change the search parameters; I had to suffer the humiliation that comes from discovering through a third party that the search had been wired all along!

Unfortunately, all my hunt for big game did was burn up my time, ruin my good name (candidates for president positions don't take kindly to being interviewed for phantom positions), and rob me of a lot of money that could've been earned doing real work for clients with sincere needs.

It was after this disaster that I decided to make a radical improvement in my search methodology. I did it by switching my focus from writing "job orders" to sending prospective clients highly detailed contracts and proposals.

Put Your Job Orders in Writing

Taken on face value, contracts and proposals are simply documents designed to prevent misunderstandings by spelling out the responsibilities of each party. However, the real value in contracts and proposals is that they allow you to:

[1] Qualify search assignments in terms of their actual viability;

[2] Gather the in-depth information you need in order to complete the assignments you determine to be workable; and

[3] Establish control as a key element in your client relationships.

In addition, contracts and proposals represent an excellent vehicle for *closing* on an order. The printed word not only creates instant credibility in the mind of the customer (your position is legitimized by virtue of the fact that everything's written down), but positions your services and fees in such a way as to be formally accepted.

Contracts and proposals also act as impersonal buffers, and can help diffuse any hard feelings or disagreements that might arise. As third-party *straw men*, they can take the heat in your place, as in, "This is our standard contract. I'm afraid I can't give you a discount."

A Word About Your Fee Schedule

If improperly used, a fee schedule can be one of the least effective forms of commercial communication, and lacks the power of either a contract or a proposal.

In fact, I try to avoid using the term "fee schedule" altogether. When communicating my fee in writing, I prefer to

63

pair the word "fee" with the word "agreement," rather than the word "schedule."

Here's why: A fee *schedule* is simply a price list, whereas a fee *agreement* requires the signature of the customer, confirming his or her consent to make payment following the receipt of services.

My feeling is, if you're going to spell out your terms and conditions to a potential customer, you might as well try to get their approval in writing at the same time. The worst that can happen is that you fail to get a signature, which in some ways might be the best thing that can happen, in that you'll spare yourself the disappointment of working on a bogus job order, or worse, prevent a collection headache from occurring down the road.

Signed or unsigned, fee schedules are difficult to enforce, because the relationship between you and the customer is hardly ever explicitly defined, and major loopholes have a way of "popping up" at the most inopportune time.

Poorly worded fee schedules, for example, rarely protect you against all-too familiar gambits, such as, "We don't owe you a fee because we already had your candidate's resume on file," or, "We heard about your candidate from someone at another division of our company."

Because of the inherent lack of reciprocal commitment, I'm not a big fan of fee schedules or fee agreements, and I send them only in situations in which additional clarification of terms is required.

From my experience, mailing or faxing 50 fee schedules a day to various tire-kickers represents nothing more than an exercise in futility. I know, because I used to do it.

A Really Decent Proposal

A proposal is more comprehensive than a fee agreement, in that it not only specifies the fee for your services, but also states precisely what it is you're going to *do* for the fee.

A proposal also contains an important feature lacking in a

fee agreement: *convertibility*.

By beefing up the specificity of a proposal and adding a line requiring the prospect's signature, your proposal instantly converts to a contract. When I deliver a proposal to a prospect or client, what I'm actually giving them is a contract in disguise.

If the customer is interested in your service, but is not yet in a position to commit, you might try writing a *pre-proposal* as a fall-back technique.

Unlike a proposal, a pre-proposal never mentions specific fees. Its purpose is to verify your understanding of the customer's needs, explain the capabilities of your service, and drop qualifying questions in the lap of the customer. In other words, it's like a job order that you submit for the client's approval.

A well written pre-proposal makes a great selling tool, in that it demonstrates, in writing, your willingness and ability to satisfy the customer's needs. Assuming both you and the customer can tie up any loose ends brought up during the pre-proposal stage, you can then proceed to the next step, either the delivery of a proposal or the signing of a contract. If you get hung up in the pre-proposal stage, at least you've gained a better understanding of the sticky issues, and you've avoided committing yourself on a price.

Contracts: The Short and Sweet of It

A contract goes even further than a proposal, in that it stipulates precise payment terms, delivery schedules, and so forth. To avoid surprises, it's best to review the content of each contract with the other party prior to getting it signed.

I write contracts that are short and sweet, rather than long and weighty. Long contracts are better suited for flaky customers who need the riot act read to them in advance (and who needs customers like that, anyway?). Long contracts generally contain extraneous negotiating points that tend to distract your customers and tie up their time and attention;

and worst of all, long contracts increase the risk that you'll paint yourself into a corner or promise to deliver more work than is really necessary.

For any repeat business you get with a client company that has your original contract on file, you can use a *follow-on contract*. This is an abbreviated document that skips all the boiler plate and gets down to the major issues at hand, namely, the nature of the search, delivery schedule, and fees. In my mind, a follow-on contract is the most gratifying symbol of a successful client/consultant relationship.

Search Navigators and Reference Interviews

Every contract or proposal I send is accompanied by a worksheet that must be filled out by the employer before the search can begin. I call this worksheet a *navigator*, because it helps steer the client and me in the direction of success.

Navigators put the onus on the hiring manager to think through and *commit to writing* the salient elements of the search. From a tactical perspective, the navigator is my way of helping the employer write the job order for me. The navigator also covers me in case of a dispute, saves me a lot of time on the phone trying to pull information out of the hiring manager, and helps clarify the parameters of the search.

Once I get the completed navigator back from the employer, I schedule a *reference interview* to cover any points that need clarification or may be missing from the navigator. When I conduct a reference interview with a client, it's analogous to the flight commander going over a final checklist with mission control prior to a space shuttle launch --- it gives me the means to abort the mission or make any necessary corrections before I take off on a flight that may be doomed. If the reference interview goes well and I've got my signed contract in hand, then the search begins.

Safety Valves and Guarantees

In any partnership in which risk is involved, it's only natural that each party will want to hedge their bets.

For example, I get very specific in my contracts about the intended position title and reporting relationships of the candidate my client wants me to find; and I always make reference to a job description and/or navigator that's been provided me by the hiring manager or HR manager.

I do this so that if the position, reporting relationship or job description changes in an unreasonable manner after the search has begun (not an uncommon occurrence), I can't be held accountable for failure to refer a "qualified" candidate.

In addition, we occasionally put a lot of honest work into filling positions that suddenly become "closed." However, by specifying provisions in our contracts such as percentage deposits, up-front engagement fees or expense reimbursement, we can protect ourselves from taking a financial bath after the client has pulled the plug.

From the employer's perspective, nothing could be worse than paying a fee, only to have the candidate quit or fail to meet expectations within the first year or two of his employment.

To assuage the fears of the employer, I recommend that they not hire anyone they fear might not work out. Beyond that, I offer a 60-day replacement guarantee, which I feel is generous, given the fact that the decision to hire is the employer's, not mine (and the search fee represents fair compensation for my services, not for the exchange of human life, a convention that was outlawed by Abraham Lincoln in 1863).

The Evolution of a Job Order

Over the years, as I've become more confident in my ability to set terms and conditions (and less willing to waste my time without some form of tangible commitment from prospective clients), my communications with prospects have evolved from telephone job orders to proposals to contracts.

The days of filling out a job order form, hanging up the phone, faxing over a fee schedule and spinning my wheels are long gone. I only wish I'd made the switch earlier.

Remember, you can't position yourself in the market without exerting some degree of control over your business. Call-in job orders, for example, used to get me really excited. Now when I receive a call-in order, I explain to employers exactly how I work, thank them for their interest, and send them a package of information about my services.

If an employer is serious and qualified, then there's a good chance we'll work together. But I can't afford to drop everything I'm doing just because a hiring manager called my office to inquire about my service.

Additional Means of Employer Control

While we're on the topic of employer control, I'd like to mention a couple of tools I've used with great success over the years.

The first is the *reference check*, one of the most effective selling devices ever invented. There are three keys to a successful reference. These include:

[1] *Timing.* A reference check is more effective when used in a proactive, rather than a reactive mode. I'd rather an employer read a dynamite reference before (or immediately following) a face-to-face or significant interview than two weeks later, when the excitement has cooled and the candidate is just one of many under consideration. In other words, strike while you have the employer's attention. By preempting the reference check, you also maintain more control over the situation.

Not long ago, I got lazy and lost a deal because I allowed the employer to call a candidate's reference before my intervention. What was really weird about the situation was the fact that the employer called the candidate's current supervisor.

Not surprisingly, the supervisor acted in his own self-interest and gave the candidate a lousy reference, hoping it would scare off the new employer, which it did, despite the fact that there were three other bona fide references who swore the candidate walked on water.

[2] *Organization.* A well organized, carefully thought out reference check format will cover all the bases, especially those issues that may be of concern to the employer. In fact, I spend the most time during a telephone reference check on specific issues that need resolution in the employer's mind. This technique is as old as the hills and is very effective. It's called "closing on the objection."

[3] *Presentation.* The reference checks I mail or fax to employers are representative of my professional service and the quality of my candidates. Therefore, I concentrate on making every reference look clean, polished and dignified.

Many times during my recruiting career, a reference check has made the difference between a placement and a near-miss.

For example, I once spoke with a reference who told me the employer would be crazy if he didn't hire the candidate. And as it later developed, the employer wasn't quite sold on my candidate, even after my reference check was delivered.

So I got on the phone with the reference and asked if he would tell the employer what he had told me. An hour later, the employer offered my candidate the job.

Signed Job Descriptions and Acceptance Confirmations

In addition to reference checks, there are a couple of other tricks of the trade that have proven invaluable over the years, both in terms of closing and preserving deals.

In today's freewheeling employment market, in which loyalty has increasingly taken a back seat to expediency, candidates are understandably touchy about the legality and enforceability of job offers.

To demonstrate the utter sincerity of the employer's intention to hire and to make good on promises made during the interviewing process, I recommend that employers provide written (and signed) job descriptions to the candidates they wish to hire.

Besides specifying the parameters of the position to be filled, these job descriptions should include, at least in general terms, some of the employer's key goals and expectations that were agreed to during the interview.

This method of solidifying the intent to hire works wonders in terms of building trust and clarifying mutual responsibilities, especially if the candidate is being offered an *upgrade* position, for which there's no formal job description or official requisition.

Whether or not you need a signed job description to seal the deal, I suggest you coach the employer on how to write an acceptance letter to the candidate. Here's what you say:

Mr. Employer, let me make a suggestion. Rather than write the candidate a letter of offer, as is customary, I'd like you to write a letter of acceptance, so that your company acknowledges in writing the candidate's acceptance of your offer.

Instead of reading, "We are pleased to make you the following offer," the letter should say, "This letter confirms your acceptance of our offer."

In my experience, this sends a more powerful statement of your commitment to the candidate's success than a standard letter of offer.

An acceptance letter is different than an offer letter, in that it discourages the candidate from using a good faith offer as a form of leverage with his current employer.

The fact that the letter confirms the candidate's acceptance, rather than a company's offer of employment, puts the candidate in a much weaker bargaining position with his old boss --- and puts you in a much stronger position to make the deal stick.

The greater the level of client commitment, the greater your income potential.

Fig. 4.1 The executive search navigator is a terrific tool for client control.

Executive Search Navigator

1. Position title:

2. Reporting relationships:

    a. direct supervisor/title

    b. indirect supervisors/titles

    c. peers/titles

    d. direct reports/titles

    e. size of department and candidate's ranking within department

3. Job function (describe a "typical" day in terms of priorities, supervisory responsibilities, most pressing concerns, etc.):

4. Expected short term results:

    (long term)

5. Expected first year cash compensation (base + bonus):

    Other benefits and/or perquisites (including medical insurance, stock, retirement, etc.):

6. Growth potential or growth expectations, in terms of position and earnings:

7. Please describe the candidate's:

    a. required product familiarity

    b. necessary technical abilities

    c. preferred educational background

    d. required managerial/supervisory responsibilities

    e. ideal personality/interpersonal qualities

8. Why is the position open? What have you done to fill it? How many candidates have you seriously considered for the position?

9. Why would someone leave their present company to work for you (product innovation, career or promotional opportunities, earning potential, technical challenge, etc.)?

10. Describe the three most viable candidates you have interviewed so far.

   • Candidate #1

      a] current position/company/salary

      b] reason your offer was not extended or was rejected

   • Candidate #2

      a] current position/company/salary

      b] reason your offer was not extended or was rejected

   • Candidate #3

      a] current position/company/salary

      b] reason your offer was not extended or was rejected

11. List five (5) companies that are likely to produce desirable candidates. (Please indicate specific divisions if more than one exists.)

   • Company   location   product

   • Company   location   product

   • Company   location   product

   • Company   location   product

   • Company   location   product

12. List any related industries, product associations or centers of technology that would qualify a candidate for this position.

13. Are there any companies to avoid in our search? Why?

14. List any specific questions that the candidate should be asked.

15. Authorization: This document was prepared by _____

   Title _____ Date _____

Fig. 4.2 A modified retained search contract.

September 30, 1994

Mr. Alan Gless
TURTLE RESOURCES, INC.
5600 Cottle Road
San Jose, CA 95193

Dear Alan:

Radin Associates welcomes the opportunity to work with you on your search. Based on our discussion of your company's needs, I am submitting the following proposal for your approval.

I. PROJECT PURPOSE AND DESCRIPTION
Through original research, Radin Associates will develop a list of qualified candidates as per your skill, educational and salary specifications. The referral information we provide will then be used by TURTLE RESOURCES to select one or more candidates to interview and ultimately, hire.

II. CANDIDATE PROFILE
A specific inventory of preferred candidate qualifications, characteristics and attributes will be determined prior to the initiation of the project (please refer to the executive search navigator).

III. STRATEGY AND EXECUTION
Candidate identification, recruitment and referral requires industry-specific original research and in-depth analysis, with relevant data obtained through published and proprietary industry sources, pre-existing research materials, and exhaustive telephone networking of target candidates. By synthesizing the information gathered, Radin Associates will be able to satisfy the following objectives:

[1]   Identify candidates whose skill sets are complementary with TURTLE RESOURCES' products, technology and customer base;
[2]   Qualify candidates by telephone screening and cross-referencing to verify the accuracy of the research sources;
[3]   Assess selected candidates for availability and interest; and
[4]   Refer only those candidates willing (or in a realistic position) to consider employment with TURTLE RESOURCES.

Pertinent data such as references and degree verification will also be included as part of the search service.

IV. PROJECT SCHEDULE
Subject to your approval, research will begin on or before Friday, October 21, 1994. In addition to our reference interview with the hiring manager, periodic telephone consultations and bench markings (your schedule permitting) will help ensure the timely exchange of pertinent information. Progress reports will be made on a weekly basis, and qualified candidates will be referred as soon as they are prescreened and available for interviewing.

V. TERMS AND CONDITIONS
The fee for the project will be one-third (33.3%) of the first year estimated salary for the position. Fees will be paid according to the following schedule:
- Deposit of one third the estimated fee (calculated at the midpoint of the salary range) due before work is initiated;
- Balance due upon start date of the referred candidate.

Telephone, electronic database access, and overnight delivery expenses will be billed separately. Expenses will be kept to a minimum, and typically average $600 per search. If the placed candidate terminates or is terminated from his or her position for any reason other than lack of work within sixty (60) days of his or her date of start, Radin Associates will find a suitable replacement within a reasonable period of time following the termination.

VI. AUTHORIZATION
Radin Associates is uniquely qualified to undertake this project. Our research capabilities, industry background, networking resources and prior experience in executive search for high-tech sensor and instrumentation companies will enable TURTLE RESOURCES to gain access to the best possible candidates with the highest degree of confidence.

Sincerely,

William G. Radin, President   Date
RADIN ASSOCIATES

Accepted By:

Alan Gless, Engineering Manager   Date
TURTLE RESOURCES, INC.

Fig. 4.3 A follow-on contract.

September 29, 1994

Mr. Vince Morrison
MIDLAND CORPORATION
430 Constitution Drive
San Jose, CA 94025

Dear Vince:

In response to your request, Radin Associates will be pleased to conduct a search similar to the one completed earlier this year for Wayne Kern. The purpose of the search will be to identify suitable candidates for the position of engineering manager, reporting to Mike Schulman.

Upon approval, the project can begin immediately. Periodic telephone consultations and bench markings will ensure the timely exchange of pertinent information.

The fee for the search project is $24,000 and will be due upon completion. Telephone, electronic database access (if required), and overnight delivery expenses will be billed separately. Expenses will be kept to a minimum, and typically average less than $600.

Radin Associates is uniquely qualified to undertake this project. Our research capabilities, industry background, networking resources and prior experience with your organization will enable MIDLAND to gain access to the best candidates with the highest degree of confidence.

Sincerely,

_____   _____
William G. Radin, President   Date
RADIN ASSOCIATES

Accepted By:

_____   _____
Vince Morrison, VP Sales   Date
MIDLAND CORPORATION

Fig. 4.4 A reference check worksheet designed for thoroughness and accuracy.

Reference Check Worksheet

Client company _____

Hiring manager _____ Title _____

  [1] Confidential reference for

  [2] Obtained from

  [3] Telephone (W)   (H)

  [4] Relationship to candidate

  [5] Dates of employment

  [6] Candidate's title

  [7] Salary/compensation

  [8] Reason for leaving

  [9] Nature of candidate's work

  [10] Number and type supervised

  [11] Candidate's strengths

  [12] Weaknesses, if any, and how the candidate worked to overcome them

  [13] How did the candidate's performance compare with similar employees?

  [14] How did the candidate get along with his supervisors and/or peers?

  [15] Describe the candidate's written and verbal communication skills

  [16] How was the candidate's work ethic and/or job attendance?

  [17] Personal problems affecting work? Would you rehire the candidate if a
       suitable position were available?

  [18] How would you comment on the candidate's likelihood for success?

  [19] Additional comments

Completed by _____ Date _____

Fig. 4.5 A completed telephone reference check.

Telephone Reference Check

Confidential reference for: William T. Crane

Date: June 28, 1994

Obtained from: Chuck Taylor, president, Quaketronix Corporation.

Telephone: (W) 805-582-1800   (H) 805-582-7361

Relationship to candidate: Direct supervisor, Quaketronix Guntersville, Alabama facility.

Dates of employment: April 1988 to June 1993.

Candidate's title: Test engineering manager.

Salary/compensation: $64,000 plus benefits.

Reason for leaving: Bill was ambitious, and felt he couldn't advance into a higher level position in Alabama. Bill later became nervous about the future of the company in the wake of revelations of fraud by Quaketronix ownership in 1992.

Nature of candidate's work: Bill performed capacity analysis and was responsible for quotes for software, fixtures, burn-in, ESS (electrical stress screening) and functional tests. After the business was awarded, his group developed the tests, built test equipment, and tested the products.

Number and type supervised: Ten to 15 engineers and technicians in Colorado Springs; up to 30 in Alabama.

Strengths: Bill is very technically oriented and understands what it takes to properly test a product. He also knows how to maximize performance of the product itself and works well with design engineers at the customer site.

4 • Increase the Level of Client Commitment

Telephone reference check, page 2

Weaknesses, if any, and how the candidate worked to overcome them:

Bill is a workaholic, which is a both a strength and a weakness. He is very hands-on, and likes to be involved with the technical details; but over time, he made a real effort to delegate more, and had some success.

How did the candidate's performance compare with others in a similar capacity?

I'd like to have him back. He was by far the best test engineering manager I've ever had the opportunity to work with. Extremely well rounded at the system as well as the component level.

How did the candidate get along with his supervisors and/or peers?

Got along fine. Always kept us up to date, was extremely personable.

Describe the candidate's written and verbal communication skills:

Made improvements in his documentation skills and became quite proficient. Had good verbal skills, was good with customers and company employees. Commanded a great deal of respect technically.

How was the candidate's work ethic and/or job attendance?

Bill was a classic workaholic; at times, we had to ask him to take a break.

Personal problems affecting work: None.

Would you rehire the candidate if a suitable position were available? Yes.

Additional comments:

Would do a fine job at Universal Gadget. Has aspirations for advancement. Bill is definitely one of the best in the business.

Reference check completed by William G. Radin

79

Fig. 4.6 A client's offer acceptance letter helps to solidify the placement.

1 September 1989

Mr. Stephen Treat
7962-L Crosshaven Drive
Dublin, OH 43026

Dear Stephen:

This letter is to confirm your acceptance of our offer of employment as Production Manager, Sensor Division. Your starting date is October 2, 1989, at an annual salary of $37,000.00.

We recognize that you have a sound background in physics and good industrial experience but that the specifics of our business will be unfamiliar. We normally regard the first three months as a probationary period, and in your case you will not have anyone reporting formally to you during that period. There is normally a formal review at six months, and thereafter annually. We are sure you will be a quick learner and begin making contributions soon, so we will play it by ear as you pick up responsibility.

Please feel free to call or make an appointment to visit prior to your start date in order to discuss our expectations or any other point of concern. Have a pleasant visit with your family.

Regards,
LAKE SHORE CRYOTRONICS, INC.

Philip R. Swinehart, Ph.D
Vice President, Sensor Division

PS/ps

cc Bill Radin

High Performance in Low Temperature Technology

64 East Walnut Street · Westerville, Ohio 43081-2399
614/891-2243 · 614/891-1392 (FAX) · 24-5415 CRYOTRON WTVL (Telex)

5

Negotiate Your Way to Higher Fees

Everything is *not* negotiable!

I recently tried to leverage one bank against the other when applying for a loan, arguing that if I couldn't get the interest rate I wanted, I was willing to walk away.

"Go ahead," the loan officer chuckled. "I've got eight other applications on my desk, waiting for approval. If you can get a better deal somewhere else, be my guest."

He's got a lot of nerve, I thought. But I sure respect the way he held the line.

Later, I found out that his bank had one of the highest ratings in the industry, and was one of the most profitable institutions in the country. And eventually, because of other value-added services, his bank became my lender, even though they had a higher rate.

Negotiating: A Way to Satisfy Needs

Price, of course, is only one aspect of any sale. If the transaction involves a *commodity* (such as rice, or soybeans, or crude oil, for example), then price may very well be the predominant issue.

Recruiters often find themselves in a position of trying to negotiate for a standard fee when others are discounting. The most successful recruiters know that the only way to offset a concern surrounding *price* is to build *value*. Otherwise, the service provided is viewed as a commodity, with the recruiter assuming the role of a vendor, or supplier.

The way to distinguish your service and its value-added dimension is to probe for the needs of the employer, and the urgency in filling a position. Once the need has been identified (and qualified), you'll be in a position to hold the line, or at least reach an agreement in which both parties feel satisfied. (If you are unable to discover a compelling reason why your service warrants the full price you charge, then unfortunately, you may have to settle for whatever you can get. This is especially true when recruiting for commodity, or rank and file candidates.)

The loan officer at my bank was able to secure my business, even though he charged a higher rate of interest than a competitor. The reason? There were other important factors that I considered to be of value that led to our settlement.

Four Steps to a Successful Settlement

You can sharpen your negotiating skills by following the four steps leading to a successful settlement.

First, *measure* what the other side wants. Before you begin negotiating, find out exactly what the employer is asking for.

I know this sounds rather obvious, but you'd be surprised how often a recruiter will "give away the store" after hearing the employer ask for a concession which is totally vague.

The plea, "Oh come on, you can do better than that!" often results in enormous and needless concessions. Finding out from the employer exactly how much better you have to do must occur before any serious discussion can take place.

Second, *qualify* the negotiation.

If the employer isn't sincere (or in a position to buy), or has completely unrealistic expectations, you shouldn't be negotiating at all.

What good does it do to settle for a reduced fee with a prospective client in the first five minutes of taking a job order only to find out later that he won't be hiring for another six weeks and that he's currently interviewing applicants from the ads he's been running?

Or, how do you handle a negotiation with an employer who wants you to fill a $60,000 a year position for a flat fee of $2,000? You don't. Move on to another prospect, or let this one know in a polite way that he's brought a baseball bat to a soccer match.

Here's an interesting story: I recently received a $15,000 search fee. Three years ago, when I made my very first marketing call to the same employer, he told me that he was only willing to pay a flat fee of one thousand dollars!

At that time, I simply let him know that I'd like to have his business, but we were so far apart that it didn't make sense to talk. He understood, I kept the lines of communication open, and finally, years later, we were able to reach an agreement, and put together a deal.

By the same token, you must be reasonably certain that your service will produce satisfactory results before you proceed in the negotiation. If you honestly feel that you can't fill your employer's position, why waste each other's time negotiating?

Third, *probe* for pertinent information.

After you know what your employer is proposing, and he is qualified to negotiate with you, try and gather every bit of information you possibly can.

What has been his previous experience with search firms? With whom has he worked? How did they operate? What did they charge? Has he been happy with the results? Why is he now talking to you? What are his expectations? What special services are important? Is price an issue? Are terms an issue? Is time an issue? What hidden forces are at play? Ego? Pride? Fear? Prestige?

In other words, take a careful look at what the employer's benefit needs are. Very often, there exists a critical hidden agenda, which will often prove to be the pivotal point of a negotiation.

You never know what secrets may be lurking behind the scenes. A decision-maker once confessed to me that the only reason he was negotiating with me was to help his personnel staff save face. Any concession, no matter how minor, he told me, would appear to be a "victory" for them. Did I help him out? Sure.

Time, Information and Power

Finally, *assess* the situation.

There are three basic underlying elements in every negotiation: time, information, and the assumption of power. Your personal inventory of needs, in the context of these elements, will enable you to make an assessment of your situation, and probable outcome.

- **Time.** What are the time considerations in this negotiation? Is anyone under the pressure of a deadline?

- **Information.** Do you know enough about the situation and everyone's needs, or are you guessing? And by the way, what does the other side know about your needs?

- **Power.** Do you have an accurate picture of the relative strength or control factors in the negotiation? Who can least afford to walk away?

Now you must probe for your own needs and agenda.

How much do you need this employer's business? What are your chances of filling his job orders? What will you gain from making concessions? What will you lose? How much anger or disappointment will result from making concessions? Do you actually need to make any concessions? If you do make concessions, what will they be?

You are now ready to reach an agreement, but remember that you can always delay if you feel you have to. It's better to put off a bad or uncomfortable deal than agree to something you'll later regret.

And it goes without saying that you should hold up your end of a deal, once you've negotiated an agreement. Nothing is more frustrating or disillusioning than an episode of bad faith negotiating. People may do it, but you should try and stick to the high road. You'll never be sorry for maintaining an elevated standard of ethics.

Negotiating a Win-Win Settlement

A while back, my wife and I dropped in on Ken, an old musician friend of mine.

Ken long ago traded his career as a piano player for the life of an entrepreneur. He sells the advertising that appears on plastic phone book covers, and he's become an excellent businessman. We hadn't seen Ken for several months, and when we arrived at his house, he eagerly led us down to the basement, which he had been feverishly remodeling. When I saw the improvements he hade made to his house, I was in shock.

"Ken, this is unbelievable," I said, as I surveyed the fully equipped recording studio with wall-to-wall carpeting. "The last time I was here, the place looked like a one-room cement box. This must have cost a fortune."

"Not really," replied Ken, with obvious pride. "See that 24-track mixing console? I traded a music store owner a big phone book cover ad for that."

"Not bad," I said.

"And see that ventilation system?" Ken pointed to the ceiling. "I had a heating and cooling company put that in free of charge, in return for a multiple insertion."

I had to admit I was impressed. "So you bartered your way to riches, so to speak."

"Right," laughed Ken. "Any time I need a piece of equipment or some sort of building supply, I just pick up the phone and cold call a store owner. I guess all those years of telephone sales paid off, since I can pretty much strike a deal on every call I make."

I was humbled. I couldn't remember ever batting a thousand. I made a mental note that it was time to brush up on my negotiating skills. Who knows, maybe someday I might want to remodel *my* basement.

What *is* Negotiating, Anyway?

The term "negotiating" often conjures up visions of hostages, or highly-paid athletes, or striking workers and their high-powered special envoys.

But in reality, we all participate in varying forms of negotiation a hundred times a day; in our family and social lives, among our coworkers, and in our business relationships.

Negotiating is simply the process of helping people get what they want. And a skillful negotiator is someone who achieves a settlement in which everyone is happy.

The way in which Ken was able to remodel his basement illustrates how an effective negotiator (or selling professional) can improve the quality of his or her life with common sense and a little ingenuity.

In our business, it's surprising to learn how many of us make needless concessions on a regular basis. These concessions can appear as discounted fees, or low-quality job orders, or the unwillingness to preclose (or disqualify) reluctant or counteroffer-prone applicants.

Such unnecessary sacrifices are usually made in the spirit of "negotiating." But making others happy at our own expense isn't negotiating; it's simply a way of avoiding the discomfort that comes from a potential disagreement, or the fear of "turning away business."

Not surprisingly, we all have a very strong tendency to "go along," even if the result is counter-productive. And sadly, the cost to us in terms of lost billings, increased anxiety, and weakened business credibility is enormous.

We have so much to gain and so little to lose by improving our negotiating skills. And the good news is that negotiating is neither painful nor difficult, once a few simple techniques have been mastered.

We Have Met the Enemy...

My high school history teacher fought in the South Pacific during World War II. He explained that during his basic military training, the U.S. soldiers were told countless stories of the savagery and courage of their Japanese opponents. The type of combat our troops were to expect would be fierce, relentless, and suicidal.

"Evidently, the Japanese were given the exact same speech by *their* drill sergeants," my teacher said. "Because the first time I came face to face with a Japanese soldier, we both practically jumped out of our skins!"

I like to relate this story to negotiating, because the "savagery" or "courage" of the other side is usually either overestimated or irrelevant. The important issues are your factual preparations, your mental attitude, and the way in which you deal with new information. Walt Kelly's cartoon character *Pogo* probably describes most negotiators when he says, "We have met the enemy, and it is us!"

So before you pull up a chair at the bargaining table, get a grip on your own needs, and what you think is at stake. A good way to begin is to examine the arithmetic behind your own fee structure, paying careful attention to the subtleties that allow many of us to "negotiate" away chunks of money we're not even aware of.

For example, I was in the business for over two years before I realized that a reduction in fee from 30 percent to 25 percent represented a discount of nearly 17 percent, not five percent. Translated into real money, on a placement of a $50,000 position, the difference is $2,500. I probably could have bought a brand new car with all the money I gave away to employers as little "five percent" discounts early in my career!

If you happen to place candidates into lower paying positions where your fee is graduated (let's say, one percent per thousand dollars of annual compensation), a one dollar difference in salary may be worth as much as $300. That's because a salary of $29,999 is worth $8,700 in fees, calculated at 29 percent; while a $30,000 salary is worth $9,000, calculated at 30 percent.

You might also make note of the fact that in terms of your billings, it takes *four* placements at a $15,000 salary to equal one placement at a $30,000 salary (using the same sliding scale method of fee calculation). Hopefully, that little factual tidbit will save you some money the next time you're dealing with a clerical employer who wants a "volume" discount.

A firm grasp of the numbers is fundamental to any successful settlement. Remember that the "funny money" syndrome --- giving away bits and pieces of seemingly insignificant money --- can cost you dearly over the long haul. After all, a thousand dollars here and a thousand dollars there can really start to add up!

The better your negotiating skills, the bigger your billings.

6

Multiply the Impact of Resumes and Cover Letters

About two or three times a year, I'll work with a really awesome candidate who totes around a totally awful resume. And if I feel there's money on the line, I'll personally rewrite the resume.

Don't misunderstand me. I'm not in the resume writing business, and neither are you. But I'll gladly spend a few minutes at my word processor to help a deserving candidate make the best possible impression on a hiring manager, especially if I think the revised resume will lead to an offer.

Reality check: The growth of information technology has demonstrably increased the importance of the resume as the principal "currency" in the employment marketplace.

Whereas a few years ago, when it was fairly easy to overcome the employer's "resume objection" with the rebuttal, "My candidate doesn't have a resume; so why don't the two of you meet Friday at 4 o'clock?" it's no longer practical to universally sidestep the resume issue.

Besides, sooner or later, your candidate will have to cough up a resume anyway, so why not come to the poker table with all your chips, ready to place your bet?

The Resume Test: Good, Better, Best

In a perfect world, only the "best suited" or "most qualified" candidate lands the job. But in the real world, it's often the best suited or most qualified *resume* that gets a candidate through the hiring manager's door for the initial interview, and ultimately influences the hiring decision.

A few years back, I learned firsthand the degree to which resume mania influences the judgment of hiring managers, and how candidates' fortunes can be affected by the visual impact of their paperwork.

Three resumes were given to me by recruited candidates who wanted to be considered for a purchasing manager position with one of my clients. All three candidates were outstanding, and had comparable backgrounds that were well-suited to my client's needs. Any one of them could have done the job the employer required, and I felt confident they would all be warmly received.

After an initial telephone presentation, during which all three candidates were found to be acceptable, my client, Walter, agreed to come into my office on a Wednesday afternoon to individually interview the candidates. However, he asked me as a courtesy to fax their resumes to him first, so that he could better prepare for the interviews.

On Tuesday, the day before the interviews, I called Walter. I was interested to know if he had had a chance to study the resumes, and if he had any questions.

Yes, he did. Would I please cancel the interview with

candidate number one?

I was puzzled. "Sure, Walter, I'll cancel it," I said. "But his ability is certainly on a par with the other two candidates. Can you tell me what leaves you cold?"

"I can't put my finger on it," he said. "I just don't think he has enough experience."

Fair enough, I thought. *He has ten years' experience as opposed to the 14 years of the other two. But he's still qualified for the job.*

"Well, how did you like the other candidates?" I asked.

"Candidate number two is better, I suppose. But I like candidate number three the best. He's got the qualifications I'm looking for."

"So, if you were to rank candidates one, two, and three in order, you'd say they were good, better, best."

"Right," said Walter. "Candidate number three is my top choice."

The Power of a Dynamite Resume

It didn't surprise me that the employer liked candidate number three the best --- he had a dynamite resume. Not only was it crammed with highly detailed information, the resume was clear, well organized, and constructed in a way that was pleasing to the eye. It left the employer with no unanswered questions regarding the candidate's education, experience and employment history. Resume number three even told the employer what products the candidate's past companies manufactured (which is an issue of paramount importance when being considered for a purchasing manager position).

In contrast, the resume of candidate number one was listless, confusing, and lacking in detail. It failed to command the reader's attention, and rambled on in a narrative style. Absent was any mention of professional achievements, such as reductions in cost or inventory; and worst of all, it was written in true (not reverse) chronological order, with the candidate's first job out of college mentioned first, not last.

Had candidate number one merely taken the time to

thoroughly reveal the full range of his experience and accomplishments (as he did with me when I interviewed him by phone), it would've been crystal clear to the employer that he was well suited to compete for the open position. But unfortunately, he failed to "sell" himself on the resume by listing his achievements, and this mistake cost him a job interview (and possibly a new job). A real tragedy, in my opinion.

Candidate number two's resume was better -- it made the cut. But it lacked the visual appeal and overall organization of resume number three. Resume number two also left a couple of key questions unanswered: What type of products did the candidate's company buy parts to make; and when did the candidate graduate from college?

And so, going into Wednesday's interviewing session, the employer had already selected a front-runner, put a second on the back burner, and eliminated a third altogether. All based solely on the impressions created by the candidates' resumes!

Play the Resume Game to Win

Of course, the resume game doesn't end with the initial selection process; it only gets more intense.

I've sat many times with decision-makers as they've culled through the finalists for an open position, and an amazing process begins to unfold. Long after the candidates have gone home, and their shining faces and brilliant interview responses have faded from memory, the manager spreads the resumes of the top candidates across his desk as if they were tarot cards.

And you know what? Nine times out of ten, after "thoughtful" consideration and a lot of head scratching, the employer selects as the front runner the candidate with the best looking resume.

Does this mean that candidates with no resumes or ugly resumes never get hired? Not at all. It happens all the time, just like people win the lottery.

But ask yourself this: If you have the means to boost your

candidates' odds of winning, why not do so?

The Tricks of the Trade

Most candidates are untrained in the art of marketing or selling themselves, especially on paper. To remedy this shortcoming, I'll occasionally spend time on the phone with an exceptional, highly placeable candidate, and make suggestions on how he can improve his resume.

But more often than not, this sort of "character building" is a waste of time --- for an outstanding candidate, it's usually easier to rewrite the resume myself.

From studying thousands of resumes and knowing the hot buttons of your client base, it's a relatively easy task for a recruiter to rework a resume into a powerful selling tool. It goes without saying, however, that it's unethical to counterfeit or "enhance" your candidates' experience.

But it is within your right to edit, reformat, and, most importantly, emphasize or expand your candidates' strongest points, especially those that you know are critical to the employer. In several memorable instances, I've made placements with candidates who would've never had the chance to interview had it not been for *resume makeovers*.

The Career Development Reports

In critical situations where time is of the essence or a fee hangs in the balance, I'll rewrite a candidate's resume. But for the rank and file, I simply don't have the time or inclination to edit resumes or counsel candidates on how to improve their paperwork.

As an alternative approach, I wrote the first of several *Career Development Reports,* entitled "How to Construct a Powerful Resume." By giving candidates an easy-to-read instructional booklet, I placed the burden of writing a dynamite resume on *their* shoulders, not mine. The *Reports* are great; they save me a lot of time, and enhance my own authority and influence with candidates by positioning myself as an "expert."

Whether I'm a true expert or not is debatable. However, I can tell you one thing: You and I know a heck of a lot more about what goes into an effective resume than 95 percent of the career counselors and professional resume writers out there, because we're in the trenches every day and we know what *works*. Our reputations and livelihoods, in fact, are often defined by the resumes of our candidates.

Serious candidates will go the extra mile to further their careers, and will eagerly take to heart any valid suggestions regarding their resumes. The information in "How to Construct a Powerful Resume" can be invaluable for resume revision, whether it's you or the candidate doing the actual work.

The Degree of Truth

Careful scrutinizing of existing resumes will help you gain an understanding of what a dynamite resume should look like. But more importantly, it can also save you a lot of trouble in identifying and dealing with resume fraud. For example, if I spot an educational credential with no date next to it, I automatically assume the candidate's falsifying his degree. Although I'd like to think of myself as a pretty trusting person, resume fraud (and our liability for it) has become all too common.

The first time I stumbled on a case of resume fraud, I was too naive (and too eager to make a placement) to realize what was happening. After all, I had no reason to suspect Ted was lying when he told me he had a master's degree in mechanical engineering. And when his alma mater said they'd never heard of him, I just assumed they'd fouled up their record keeping. Little did I imagine the wild goose chase that lay ahead.

"Ted, this is Bill calling. I contacted Cal State Long Beach, and they can't find your paperwork anywhere," I reported.

"I can't imagine why not," Ted answered. "Did you call the physics department?"

"Well, no; why should I? Your degree is in mechanical engineering."

"No, no, no. My degree is in physics."

"But you said on your resume it was in mechanical engineering."

"Oh." Ted paused. "Well, they merged the departments. Mechanical engineering's now a part of the physics department."

"Okay, Ted. I'll talk to the physics department."

But of course, they hadn't heard of him either.

"Gosh, I don't know what the problem is," Ted replied when I called him back. "Maybe they have my last name misspelled."

So I tried again, this time using five or six alternate spellings. No luck.

"Well, let's try giving them my social security number," Ted suggested. "That should do it."

But it didn't. By now I was getting a tad suspicious.

"Relax, Bill. The reason you haven't been able to track down my degree is because I got it from the classes I attended at night school. They're kept in a different file."

Oh, sure, that explains it, I thought. So I called the continuing education department. Nothing.

"Ted, I'm a little concerned." I could no longer conceal my irritation. "I must have talked to a dozen different people at Cal State Long Beach, and not a soul has ever heard your name. What's more, my client company's getting nervous. They can't extend you an offer until we can verify your degree."

"Wait a minute," Ted shot back. "Did you say Cal State Long Beach? Boy, I'm sorry, there must be a typo on my resume. I got my degree from Long Beach State."

I was beginning to smell a rat. But I wanted to give Ted the benefit of the doubt, so I got on the horn to Long Beach State, and we went through the whole thing again -- with exactly the same result.

"My friend, I'm going to need some straight answers," I said. "If you can't verify your degree, I'm afraid any deal with my client is off."

"Gee, Bill, I was meaning to tell you all along." Ted lowered his voice to a whisper. "I don't actually have a degree. I have the equivalent of a degree."

"Oh, that's just great!" I shouted. Boy, was I mad! "Do you mind telling me exactly how many credits you have from Long Beach State, or Cal State, or wherever you said you went to school?"

"Credits? Well, uh, the truth is," stuttered Ted, "I don't have any real credits. When I moved to Los Angeles a few years ago, I stopped by a local university, and someone at the front desk told me I had the same work experience as if I had a master's..."

I could have wrung his neck! Not only did he cost me a placement and spoil my reputation with a client, he made a fool of me as well. From then on, I vowed to check references before I invested my time helping a candidate get a job.

Arm Your Candidates with Custom Cover Letters

Employers get pitched on candidates all the time by recruiters, and tend to build up a certain amount of sales resistance, especially after hearing about "great" candidates ten times a day.

For additional ammunition, I sometimes use a candidate's cover letter to support a telephone presentation made on behalf of the candidate.

I don't use just *any* cover letter, though. To achieve maximum firepower, I help the candidate script a *customized* cover letter extolling his or her unique benefits in a way that fits the job description as I know it.

In a situation in which I'm marketing a candidate and there's no formal job description, I make sure to ask the employer to describe the essential skills necessary for a candidate's success, or an overview of the problems facing the employer, and what sort of person might offer a solution.

Once I know the most urgent needs of the employer (or the concerns he may have expressed towards my candidate's abilities), I can then help the candidate construct a letter that describes his fit with the company or diffuses the concerns of the employer.

Sent as an introduction to the resume, the custom cover letter reinforces the candidate's "fit," and impresses on the employer the degree to which the candidate will fight for the chance to interview.

In effect, the letter helps grease the skids for the candidate, and helps eliminate any barriers or objections the employer may have.

Cover Letter Design and Strategy

Make sure the candidate's cover letter is short and to the point, and is addressed to you, not the employer. The letter should state the candidate's interest in the position as you've described it to him, and make a strong case for why it would be in everyone's best interest to arrange an interview. Immediately upon your receipt of the letter, it should be faxed to the employer, and followed up with a phone call.

In all the years I've used this technique, it's never failed to get the candidate an interview, which is, after all, the point. In essence, you're placing the burden of proof on the candidate, not yourself, which saves you time and diminishes your role as the "seller" in the eye of the perpetually wary employer. By assuming the role of a *facilitator* rather than a salesperson, you not only boost your own credibility, but also that of the candidate.

On page 99, I've re-created a custom cover letter written to me by a candidate I placed as Director of Engineering for a small, high tech company in Seattle.

The owner/founder of the company was a Stanford Ph.D. who was reluctant to interview the candidate after my initial presentation. It seems he was concerned with two things: 1] the candidate's technical breadth (she possessed a mere MSEE Cum Laude from Vanderbilt University); and 2] her ability to excel in the entrepreneurial setting of a small company.

As you can see, the employer's concerns were answered very eloquently by the candidate, who loaded up the letter with as much techno-jargon as she could, so as to leave no doubt as to her technical wizardry.

This fine work by the candidate led to an immediate interview (and subsequent hire) following my fax transmittal of her cover letter to the employer.

Remember, many candidates will neither need nor benefit from your help. But in certain cases,

The effort you spend on resume makeovers and custom cover letters will pay enormous dividends.

Fig. 6.1 A powerfully written custom cover letter.

December 20, 1994

Mr. Bill Radin
Radin Associates
via fax: (505) 983-2243

Dear Mr. Radin:

I enjoyed talking with you on the phone Friday and receiving from you the job specification for the engineering manager position. As we discussed on the phone, I have much relevant experience in product development and project management applied to industrial instrumentation and systems development.

Specifically in the area of camera-based instrumentation, I have been a user (infrared scanning of casting and rolling operations), research manager (development of perforation, streak-detection and scanning-colorimetry monitors for United States Postage Stamps), and developer (residual trash-in-cotton instrument) of image processing applications.

My technical background is rather broad. As noted in the accompanying resume, I have worked the range from basic sensor interfaces, through embedded microprocessors and DSP, up to computer-based information networks. I am at home with analog/digital and hardware/software design activities.

However, I feel my chief business contribution comes from my competency in the management of the innovation/new business development process. In this regard, I can formulate development goals from an understanding of the marketplace, overall business goals, and technical possibilities; assemble and motivate a team to achieve these goals; and integrate the technology development into the overall business. My recent experience has been with a very lean organization, and I understand the advantages of simplicity, out-sourcing and speed.

I hope this additional information is of use in evaluating my background for this and other positions.

Regards,

Randi E. Lorber
400 Logan Court
Knoxville, TN 37945

Fig. 6.2 A poorly-designed resume that was totally overhauled.

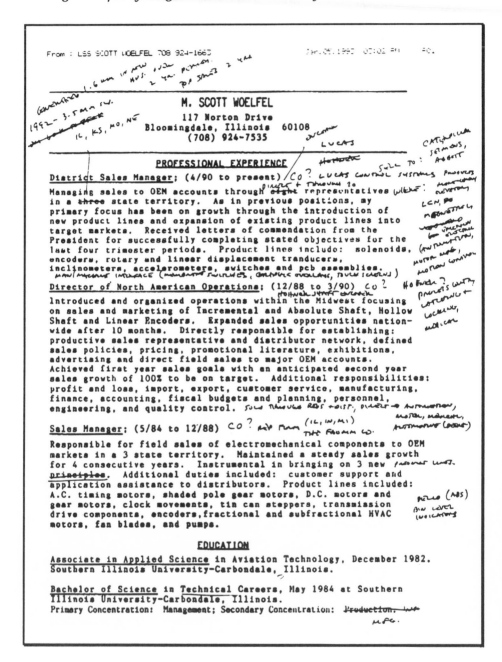

Fig. 6.3 The "new" version that led to a director-level placement.

M. SCOTT WOELFEL
117 Norton Drive
Bloomingdale, IL 60108
(708) 924-7535

Objective   Sales and/or marketing position in which my self-motivation and new business development skills are fully utilized.

Experience   Lucas Control Systems Products   1990 to present
Manufacturer of solenoids, encoders, rotary and linear displacement transducers, inclinometers, switches, PCB assemblies, and man/machine interface devices
District Sales Manager
Responsible for the introduction of new product lines and expansion of existing lines into automotive, motion control, process control, and medical target markets. Customers include Caterpillar, Magnetrol, Siemens, Abbott, LCN, and Emerson Electric. Manage sales to OEM accounts directly and through 20 manufacturers' representatives in a four state Midwest region.
- Generated $1.6 million in new business over a two-year period.
- Achieved individual 1992 sales production of $3.5 million.
- Produced 28% of total optical encoder product line revenue out of a sales force of 22.

Hohner Shaft Encoders   1988 to 1990
International manufacturer of incremental and absolute shaft, hollow shaft, and linear encoders
Director of North American Operations
Introduced and organized North American sales. Responsible for establishing a productive sales representative and distributor network. Defined sales policies, pricing, promotional literature, exhibitions, advertising, and direct field sales to major OEM accounts in automotive, motor, medical, and automation markets. Additional responsibilities included profit and loss, import, export, customer service, and manufacturing, engineering, and quality control in the Toronto and Chicago plants.

The Fromm Company   1984 to 1988
Manufacturers' representative firm with product lines including AC timing motors, shaded pole gear motors, DC motors and gear motors, clock movements, tin can steppers, transmission drive components, encoders, fractional and subfractional HVAC motors, pumps, and fan blades
Sales Manager
Responsible for field sales of electromechanical components to OEM markets in a three-state territory. Instrumental in adding three new product lines to the firm. Additional duties included customer support and application assistance to distributors.

Education   Southern Illinois University
B.S. Technical Careers. Concentration in management and manufacturing, 1984
A.S. Applied Science, Aviation Technology, 1982

References   Available upon request.

Fig. 6.4 A few of the Career Development Reports (see chapters 6, 7 and 8).

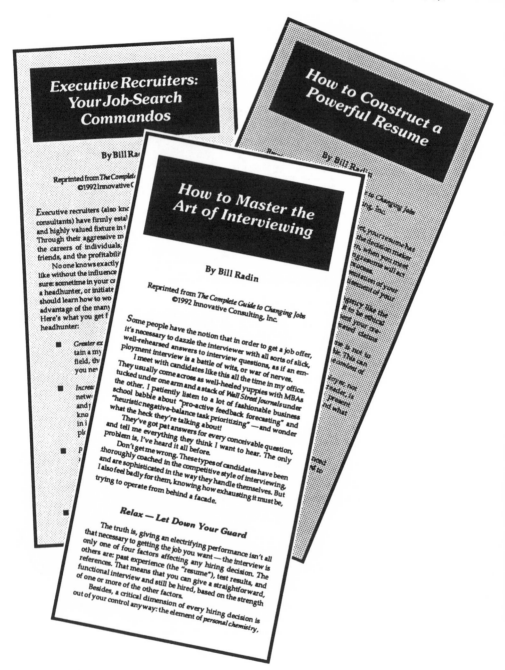

**Executive Recruiters:
Your Job-Search
Commandos**

By Bill Ra[...]

Reprinted from *The Complet[...]*
©1992 Innovative C[...]

Executive recruiters (also kno[...]
consultants) have firmly esta[...]
and highly valued fixture in [...]
Through their aggressive m[...]
the careers of individuals, [...]
friends, and the profitabili[...]
   No one knows exactly [...]
like without the influence [...]
sure: sometime in your c[...]
a headhunter, or initiate [...]
should learn how to wo[...]
advantage of the many [...]
Here's what you get f[...]
headhunter:

   ■   *Greater ex[...]*
       tain a m[...]
       field, th[...]
       you ne[...]

   ■   *Increa[...]*
       netw[...]
       and j[...]
       kno[...]
       in i[...]
       pl[...]

   ■   *P[...]*
       [...]

**How to Construct a
Powerful Resume**

By Bill Radin

**How to Master the
Art of Interviewing**

By Bill Radin

Reprinted from *The Complete Guide to Changing Jobs*
©1992 Innovative Consulting, Inc.

Some people have the notion that in order to get a job offer,
it's necessary to dazzle the interviewer with all sorts of slick,
well-rehearsed answers to interview questions, as if an employment interview is a battle of wits, or war of nerves.
   I meet with candidates like this all the time in my office.
They usually come across as well-heeled yuppies with MBAs
tucked under one arm and a stack of *Wall Street Journals* under
the other. I patiently listen to a lot of fashionable business
school babble about "pro-active feedback forecasting" and
"heuristic negative-balance task prioritizing" —and wonder
what the heck they're talking about!
   They've got pat answers for every conceivable question,
and tell me everything they think I want to hear. The only
problem is, I've heard it all before.
   Don't get me wrong. These types of candidates have been
thoroughly coached in the competitive style of interviewing,
and are sophisticated in the way they handle themselves. But
I also feel badly for them, knowing how exhausting it must be,
trying to operate from behind a facade.

Relax — Let Down Your Guard

   The truth is, giving an electrifying performance isn't all
that necessary to getting the job you want — the interview is
only one of four factors affecting any hiring decision. The
others are: past experience (the "resume"), test results, and
references. That means that you can give a straightforward,
functional interview and still be hired, based on the strength
of one or more of the other factors.
   Besides, a critical dimension of every hiring decision is
out of your control anyway: the element of *personal chemistry,*

102

7

Control Your Candidates and Expand Your Income

Like any other professional service that deals with the public, recruiters continuously struggle with the issue of control. The same way doctors wrestle with "patient control" and lawyers boast about "client control," so recruiters agonize over "candidate control."

If you look at our business realistically, you'll recognize that you can no more "control" the actions of another person than you can control a speeding vehicle that's hydroplaning down the interstate at 60 miles an hour in a driving rain. That is, the force of momentum will to a greater or lesser degree affect the direction your candidate takes, just like it will a 3,000 pound car. The best you can hope for is that you've selected the right vehicle for the trip and that your preparation, training and reflexes will guide you safely towards your destination. Your degree of control, in other words, is relative to a variety of external factors.

A Piece of Gold, Not a Lump of Coal

Does that mean that you should throw up your hands and abdicate control completely? Not at all. If anything, you should make every effort to establish and maintain control as early and often as possible. The greater your control over candidates, the greater your income potential will be, for the simple reason that you'll eliminate the time-wasters from your life.

To standardize the candidate selection process, I've developed a list of qualifying questions that help me distinguish a piece of gold from a lump of coal. Standardization is important because it gives us the means to be objective in our assessment of a candidate's worth relative to the recruiting business. The worst thing you can do is fall in love with a candidate (figuratively, that is) and launch a crusade on his or her behalf.

Naturally, a candidate's true worth depends largely on market forces, and often can't be determined until you've made several presentations. Just remember that if no one's interested in your candidate after half a dozen presentations or two or three interviews, you're probably prodding a dog that won't hunt.

Categorized in terms of the candidate's *skills, values* and *commitment,* the set of qualifying questions I've designed are intended to give me a better understanding of the candidate's makeup; and most importantly, ferret out any candidate who's a probable waste of time. Here's how I define the terms:

- **Skills** relate to the name, rank and serial number issues that define a candidate. From the most general terms (when stockpiling candidates in your industry) to the most specific (when you're qualifying candidates for a particular job order), the skills will provide you with the candidate's basic profile.

- **Values** relate to the motivating factors behind a candidate's decision to seek or not seek a new position. Values define the candidate's professional interests, aspirations, personal needs, hobbies, lifestyle preferences, family values, health and safety concerns, and so forth. If skills deal with the candidate's what issues, then values deal with the why.

- **Commitment** relates to the degree of partnership you can achieve with the candidate, plus his or her sense of urgency and likelihood of taking action. By quantifying the candidate's level of commitment, you'll get a grip on tangible issues such as the candidate's job search timeline, fear of change, counteroffer susceptibility, and acceptance of your ground rules.

Commitment questions can also provide the candidate with a reality check. I worked with an inexperienced candidate once who thought it was reasonable and customary for an employer to wait six weeks after the offer was made while the candidate "thought it over." Once I brought reality into the picture, it became clear that the candidate was a tire-kicker, since he wouldn't budge from his original expectation. Needless to say, I dropped him like a hot potato.

Each of these qualifying areas are important, and in some ways are independent of one another. A candidate that's a "dream" according to his skills, for example, may turn out to be a nightmare to work with if he's totally indifferent to making a change. Likewise, a candidate with marginal skills may turn out to be a terrific candidate because of an external factor such as relocatability.

Rapport: Getting a Grip on the Basics

If I have 15 minutes to interview a candidate, I'll try to spend five minutes on skills, five minutes on values, and five minutes on commitment. The reason: I want to qualify the candidate before investing my time.

Believe it or not, I've placed many candidates over the years without really knowing anything about them, just the basics in terms of their skills, values and commitment. Rarely do I get chummy with candidates. In fact, if I find our relationship leaning in that direction, more often than not, I'm dealing with a person I have little chance of placing.

Rapport, in my opinion, can be established much more quickly by asking probing, qualifying questions than by talking about the candidate's preferences in presidential politics, chili recipes or ski resorts. A little bit of schmoozing is fine, but by demonstrating your professional ability to zero in on what's important to the candidate, you're automatically building credibility, gaining (and demonstrating) respect, and establishing control.

Qualifying Questions
Concerning Values

I've found that people experience dissatisfaction with their employment situation due to one or more of the following reasons:

[1] *Personal.* The candidate's relationships with those at work are unfulfilling. Perhaps the peers and/or supervisors are incompatible with the candidate, or they have different goals. Or maybe there are vast differences in political, religious, socioeconomic or educational backgrounds. Or the overall corporate culture seems out of sync to the candidate, or the "feel" or "look" of the

company's surroundings leaves something to be desired.

I worked with a managerial candidate once who wouldn't even consider a job in Utah, because of his perception that as a "gentile," he, his wife and young children would never be accepted by a predominately Mormon culture.

[2] *Professional.* The candidate's ability to achieve career goals or technical fulfillment is stalled, or unattainable. As recruiters, it's on the professional aspects of a candidate's employment equation that we most often (and erroneously) focus our attention.

[3] *Situational.* The candidate's dissatisfaction has nothing to do with the personal or professional aspects of the job; rather, the dissatisfaction is tied to circumstances. For example, the candidate's commuting distance might be intolerable, or the air quality or school system in the candidate's city might have deteriorated; or the candidate's spouse might have recently accepted a job in a different city.

The point is, there may be a hundred different value-related reasons behind a candidate's discontent. It's your job to keep your eyes open, and see if you can prompt a response from the candidate that will reveal the true key to his or her discontent (and ultimately, offer a solution).

When probing to understand a candidate's values, it's best to ask open-ended questions, such as "What's most important to you in a job?" or "If you could change any aspect of your work (or your life), what would it be?" These are usually more effective than a rating or prioritizing system in which you might ask, "What's most important to you in a job? Is it money, autonomy or advancement?"

Never Underestimate the Power of Values

To demonstrate the importance of values in our candidates' decision-making process, consider the following:

- I witnessed a job-seeker turn down a position because he was an amateur athlete and he didn't like the air quality where my client company was located.

- Not long ago, I placed a candidate who was a long distance runner. He took the position largely because his new boss was also a runner, and would understand his need to take off work twice a year to run the New York City and Boston marathons.

- I arranged for an engineer to take a job with a company that offered him a demotion, since being highly visible within his current employer's department made him feel uncomfortable.

- I helped a radar engineer change to a lower paying job. The reason? The engineer was a member of the Olympic rowing team, and the new company was near a river.

- A recruiter I know found an excellent job for a chemist who was also an avid taxidermist. At the last minute, the chemist turned down the job, which would have required his relocation from Utah to northern California. The chemist explained that the climate in California was unsuitable for stuffing ducks.

Later, the recruiter discovered the duck-stuffer's true reason for turning down the new job. It seems he had a hometown mistress, and he couldn't convince her to relocate to California with him. The point is, every candidate has a highly personal motivation that influences his career choices.

Gathering Evidence

The ability to understand what's truly important to a candidate requires a great deal of practice. Take a look at some of these commonly used expressions, and ask yourself what they mean:

"I'm looking for a job that offers more *security*."
or
"I wish there were more *management* opportunities here."
or
"My company doesn't give me the *resources* I need."
or
"Maybe a new job would give me more *challenge*."

As recruiters, we hear word patterns like these from candidates on a regular basis. Although the motivation behind them may be sincere, the meaning is often cloudy, since the definition of a word or phrase may vary, depending on the individual or the situation.

For example, "security" to one person may mean protection from a layoff; while to another, it might signify coverage by the company pension or health insurance plan. To a third, "security" could imply that a particular job function or reporting relationship is static, and will never change.

I interviewed a candidate once who described the *challenge* she was looking for in a job as the opportunity to play third base on her company softball team. To another candidate, *greater participation* referred to his interest in deciding which manager would sit atop the dunk-tank at the annual company picnic.

When candidates tell me they're looking for *more money*, my antennae always perk up. I've learned to immediately fire back, "How much money do you mean, exactly?" since the answer I get can range anywhere from a two percent increase to part ownership in the company.

.

Getting to the Bottom Line

To avoid ambiguity in your search for a candidate's values, you can use a question-and-answer methodology psychologists call an *evidentiary procedure*. This technique will help sharpen your own self-awareness.

The candidate you're working with, for example, tells you that she wants more responsibility than she's currently getting. That's fine, except the term *responsibility* by itself is too vague. To really pinpoint the values you need to satisfy, you could ask the candidate these types of questions:

- Exactly how would you *define* responsibility?

- What *changes* would occur in your job if you were given more responsibility?

- How would you describe the *function* of someone you know who currently has the responsibility you're seeking?

- What tangible *benefits* are connected with having greater responsibility? Money? Position title? Perks, such as a company car, a private office, or a health club membership?

By forcing yourself to gather tangible evidence, you'll not only avoid wasting your time (and that of your candidates and clients); you'll be able to make a better match for every party in the employment picture. And best of all, when a prospective employer asks, "Why is your candidate looking for a new position?" you'll actually know how to respond.

Commitment: Some Closed-Ended Questions

In contrast to value questions, commitment questions should be specific and closed-ended. Here are a few examples:

- *Are you currently in the exploration, interviewing, or consideration stage with any companies? If so, what is your status at this time, and what do you anticipate will happen?*

- *Can you think of anything that would prevent you from changing jobs at this time?*

- *Exactly when will you be able to interview?*

- *How many companies will you need to interview with (or how many offers will you need) before you can make a decision to accept an offer?*

- *When will you be free and clear to start a new job? How much notice will you need to give your current employer?*

- *What is the minimum salary you would consider to be acceptable?*

- *Are there any geographic locations that you would prefer or would need to rule out? Why?*

- *Are there any employers that you would prefer or would need to rule out? Why?*

- *What would you do if you accepted a new position in good faith and your present company offered you more money to stay? Has this ever happened to you before? What was the result?*

111

The last series of questions, of course, are designed to cover the counteroffer issue. Counteroffers represent the ultimate measure of a recruiter's control, or lack thereof.

While many recruiters believe that you can reason, berate or shame a candidate out of accepting a counteroffer, I have a different philosophy.

Commitment and the Counteroffer

My experience has shown that the earlier the counteroffer issue is covered with the candidate, the better for everyone. If he or she is predisposed to take one, has a history of accepting counteroffers, or is deliberately using your service or your client company's offer as a career-leveraging device, then nothing you're going to do or say (short of blackmail) will change the situation. If, on the other hand, the candidate is predisposed *not* to take a counteroffer (based on the answers you hear while acquainting yourself with the candidate), then your counteroffer speech won't have any effect, either --- it'll be unnecessary.

If the candidate is inexperienced or uninformed about the perceived hazards of a counteroffer, then it's worthwhile to discuss the issue, in order to plant the seeds for future counteroffer rejection.

Notice, however, that I used the term *perceived* hazards. Recent industry surveys (including some by search firms) have revealed that a candidate who accepts a counteroffer stands a reasonable chance of re-establishing a productive and long-term relationship with the original employer. The notion that a counteroffer acceptance will automatically end a candidate's career is, I'm afraid, contrary to the facts.

Sadly, for all of us who've ever suffered through the heartburn of accepted counteroffers, the candidate's tactic of playing one employer against another often works, and there's really very little you can do about it once the deed is done.

Therefore, I'd much rather disqualify counteroffer-prone

candidates up front than try to scare them into submission with the argument that they're risking the destruction of their careers by accepting a counteroffer. People act in their own self-interest. By haranguing them, you'll only be wasting your time and making yourself look self-serving.

If you're faced with a situation in which you have nothing to lose, the counteroffer scare tactic can be used as a last resort --- but it may not be any more effective than closing the barn door after the horses have left.

Counteroffer Counter-Tactics

Fortunately, you're not entirely defenseless on the counteroffer battlefield. Depending on the stage at which your search has evolved, there are three practical ways to counter the counteroffer:

[1] *Disqualify the candidate.* If he or she answers the question, "What would you do if your present employer offers you more money to stay?" with, "I'd have to think it over," or, "I guess it would depend on what they offer," then you're headed for trouble, and your best bet may be to work with a different candidate.

[2] *Withhold the offer.* If your candidate admits that he's been discussing your client company's offer with his direct supervisor, or inexplicably begins to raise the ante (as in, "Gee, I'm not sure I can accept any offer unless it provides dental coverage for my dog"), then you know there's a counteroffer being orchestrated by the candidate. At this point, you should confront the candidate and, if necessary, withhold or even withdraw the offer until you feel comfortable with the outcome.

[3] *Diffuse the inevitable.* The best way to shield your

candidate from the inevitable mixture of emotions surrounding the act of resigning is to remind him that employers always follow a predictable pattern when faced with a subordinate's resignation.

The script I use with a candidate prior to his resignation goes something like this:

Mr. Candidate, turning in your resignation can be very tough emotionally. Just remember, though, that there's a three stage pattern of behavior that all managers go through:

> *[1] They'll be in shock. "You sure picked a fine time to leave! Who's going to finish the project?"*

The implication is that you're irreplaceable. They might as well ask, "How will we ever get the work done without you?"
To answer this assertion, you can reply, "If I were run over by a truck on my way to work tomorrow, I feel that somehow, this company would survive."

> *[2] They'll start to probe. "Who's the new company? What sort of position did you accept? What are they paying you?"*

Be careful not to disclose too much information, or appear too enthusiastic. Otherwise, you run the risk of feeding your current employer with ammunition he can use against you later, such as, "I've heard some pretty terrible things about your new company" or, "They'll make everything look great until you actually get there. Then you'll see what a sweat shop that place really is."

> *[3] They'll make you a counteroffer to try and keep you from leaving. "You know that raise you and I were talking about a few months back? I forgot to tell you: We were just getting it processed yesterday."*

To this you can respond, "Gee, today you seem pretty concerned about my happiness and well-being. Where were you yesterday, before I announced my intention to resign?"

It may take several days for the three stages to run their course, but believe me, sooner or later, you'll find yourself engaged in a conversation similar to this.

If your client company wants to get in a bidding war, or you don't mind living on the edge with every deal, then go ahead and work with a counteroffer-prone candidate. In my opinion, life's too short for this type of nonsense.

Extracting the Most Information in the Least Amount of Time

Most recruiters use some sort of data sheet (or the electronic equivalent) for gathering, storing, filing and retrieving essential candidate information. Whatever format you use, be sure to modify it so you can easily assess and record the skills, values and commitment of each candidate.

Aside from internal data sheets, here are a few time-saving tools that I use:

- **Resumes.** With scanning technology and optical character recognition (OCR) software, resumes can be shrunk to a digestible size for later retrieval and study. Resumes, of course, deal primarily with skills.

- **Applications.** These are great in that they not only provide you with a lot of information (again, mostly skill-related) about the candidate, they also make recruiting easier. A cleverly designed application will ask the candidate to provide you with the names of references, supervisors, past employers and peers.

- **Skill summaries.** These are forms to be filled out

115

by the candidate. Designed to evaluate the person's technical proficiency, skill summaries take the "20 questions" drudgery out of discovering a candidate's obvious and hidden abilities.

- **Self-evaluations.** These subjective first-person proclamations give the candidate a chance to freely express his accomplishments, management skills, organizational skills and personal qualities. Remember, though, that you and the employer are the ultimate judges of employment suitability, not the candidate.

- **Job search navigators.** These forms are similar to the executive search navigators, and they're very useful in the way they distill candidates down to their most basic essence in terms of skills, values and commitment. Best of all, the candidates fill out the navigators, not you.

Each of these devices serves the purpose of saving you the time you might otherwise spend talking face-to-face or over the phone. This sort of efficiency can be especially valuable when dealing with call-in candidates or "file" candidates who may be useful later but whose current value is either nil or yet to be determined. Once you've established the need to expand your knowledge of a particular candidate, you can build on the foundation laid by the form or forms you've used to gather basic data.

The Power of Third-Party Validation

To most people, job changing is an overwhelming and often frightening experience. In fact, one of the reasons I wrote the *Career Development Reports* was to help my candidates deal with the major obstacles and protocol issues surrounding the job changing process.

Covering topics such as overcoming the fear of change, mastery of the interviewing process, resume construction and the proper way to resign, the *Reports* provide candidates with valuable information, while at the same time boosting my credibility. And as with all of the written materials, they save me the time I might otherwise need to spend in lengthy conversation.

Other materials I've given to candidates have included salary surveys, cost of living surveys and article reprints (yes, even Paul Hawkinson's famous *Counteroffer Acceptance Road to Career Ruin*).

I've found that candidates are usually receptive to third-party validation. For example, if a candidate is considering a new position that will require a relocation, I have a Century 21 or Re/Max agent call the candidate to discuss housing in the new location prior to the first interview.

Writing the Candidate's Letters

Taking candidate control one step further, I usually dictate or provide sample copies of any letters I want the candidate to send my clients. Even though a thank-you letter is considered a professional courtesy, in today's market, a poorly conceived letter could potentially damage the positive impression your candidate might have created during a recent interview.

Here are five (often fatal) mistakes candidates make when writing their own thank-you letters:

[1] *Failure to proofread.* A spelling error or typo does absolutely nothing to improve the company's impression of your candidate.

[2] *Calling attention to an area of concern.* For example, the candidate writes, "I feel strongly that my customer service background will be a tremendous asset to the company." For all he knows, the company liked everything about him

except his customer service background.

[3] *Apologizing for the way he or she interviewed.* "Sorry I made such a fool of myself yesterday," your candidate writes. "I'm ordinarily pretty good with numbers."

[4] *Begging for the job.* "If you just give me a chance, I promise you'll never regret it."

[5] *Bragging about his or her abilities, or criticizing the competition.* "It should be obvious from our meeting that I'm clearly more qualified than the other candidates you interviewed."

If you dictate a thank-you letter for your candidate, you can avoid the pitfalls. Make sure your candidate uses a high quality typewriter or word processor, and by all means, make the letter as brief and antiseptic as possible.

Don't Forget the Resignation

A word about resignation letters: Although a candidate's resignation should be handled in person, a well-written letter provides everyone involved with clear confirmation (and documentation) of the event.

Keep your candidate's resignation letter short, simple and to the point. There's no need to go into detail about the new job, or what led to the decision to leave. If these issues are important to the old employer, he'll schedule an *exit interview* for the candidate, at which time the two of them can hash out their differences ad infinitum.

By the way, I would be remiss if I didn't remind you of your professional obligation to follow up with both the candidate and the employer on a regular basis after a placement has been made.

The "burn-in" period following an accepted offer is

emotionally charged with respect to the candidate's sense of anticipation, shifting loyalties, feelings of guilt, and so on.

To protect the placement you worked so hard to achieve (and to assure the employer and the candidate of their wise decision in the face of predictable buyers' remorse), you should do everything you can to focus the candidate away from his old situation and squarely towards the new.

It Ain't Over 'til It's Over

Once the candidate has started in the new job, you also need to track his learning curve and emotional adjustment to his new surroundings. If for any reason you suspect that there are problems of any kind, either personal or job-related, then by all means have a heart-to-heart with the candidate and keep the hiring manager apprised of the situation.

I recently placed a candidate from Austin, Texas into a high tech position with a company in Boulder, Colorado. Everyone involved, including the candidate, the employer and myself, knew there was a cost of living differential between the two cities; but all of us thought the issue had been resolved during a house hunting trip the candidate made prior to his acceptance of the offer.

At eight in the morning on the candidate's first day on the job, he walked into the HR manager's office and announced that he and his wife couldn't find affordable housing, and that he would have to resign.

Thinking quickly, the HR manager called a trusted real estate agent who dashed over to the company, picked up the candidate, and drove him out to look at a suburban housing development that was relatively affordable.

That afternoon, the candidate and his wife made an offer on a house, and by the following morning, the candidate was back on the job.

As you might expect, I spent that day back in my office, helplessly biting my nails, wondering if a fall-off was in the works --- which it would have been were it not for the HR manager's swift intervention.

The point is, it ain't over 'til it's over. And many times, your conscientious follow-up will save a deal from falling apart --- but only if you keep your eye on the ball.

**The more you can control
the behavior of your candidates,
the more you'll expand your income.**

Fig. 7.1 A concise, yet effective, post-interview thank-you letter.

David S. Nelson
3122 South Palm Avenue
Sierra Madre, CA 91436
(818) 984-3378

November 1, 1994

Mr. Chip Jones, General Manager
VIRGINIA BUSINESS
411 East Franklin Street, Suite 105
Richmond, VA 23219

Dear Mr. Jones:

Thank you for spending time with me last Tuesday. I feel our meeting was productive, and that I was able to gain a clear understanding of the needs of your department, and the responsibilities of the Managing Editor position you wish to fill.

The opportunity with VIRGINIA BUSINESS appears to be very exciting, and I am certain my background would represent a positive addition to your managerial staff.

If you have any further questions concerning my professional qualifications or educational credentials, please do not hesitate to call.

Sincerely,

David Nelson

cc: Mel Yudkin, VP Human Resources
        Bill Radin, Radin Associates

Fig. 7.2 A job search navigator can chart a course for placement activity.

Job Search Navigator

Candidate _____ Date _____

Current employer _____ Position _____

• Directions: Please complete the following questionnaire as thoroughly and accurately as possible. All data will be kept strictly confidential.

1. Your current position title:

2. Your direct supervisor/title:

    indirect supervisors/titles:

    peers/titles:

    direct reports/titles:

3. Your job function (describe a "typical" day in terms of priorities, supervisory duties, most pressing concerns, etc.):

4. Last year's cash compensation (base + bonus):

    Other benefits and/or perquisites (including medical insurance, stock, retirement, etc.):

5. Growth potential or growth expectations with your current employer, in terms of position and earnings:

6. Please describe your:

    a. product familiarity

    b. technical skills

    c. educational background

    d. managerial/supervisory skills

    e. personality/interpersonal style

7. Why are you seeking another position?

    What have you done to find another job?

8. What would most attract you to another company (technical challenge, career opportunities, earning potential, location, lifestyle, etc.)?

9. If you could change any aspect of your work, what would it be?

10. What have you done (or will you do) to improve the situation with your current employer?

11. Describe the "ideal" job in terms of location, company size, salary, position, start date, growth potential, or any other element that you feel will lead to satisfaction.

12. List the two (2) most recent companies you have interviewed with.

   • Company, location   Interview date(s)

     a. position, responsibilities

     b. action pending (explain)

   • Company, location   Interview date(s)

     a. position, responsibilities

     b. action pending (explain)

13. List three (3) additional companies that are likely or suitable places of employment. (Please indicate specific divisions if more than one exists.)

   • Company   location   product

   • Company   location   product

   • Company   location   product

14. List any other industries, product associations or centers of technology that might qualify a company for your consideration.

15. Are there any companies to avoid in our search? Why?

16. List any specific questions that prospective employers should be asked.

17. Can you think of anything that would prevent you from changing jobs at this time (such as an ongoing project, merger, loss of benefits, impending promotion, etc.)?

Fig. 7.3 A well-written resignation letter can diffuse a counteroffer attempt.

David S. Nelson
3122 South Palm Avenue
Sierra Madre, CA 91436
(818) 984-3378

January 1, 1995

Mr. Bruce Keir, Managing Editor
CALIFORNIA COMMERCE WEEKLY
7698 Colorado Blvd., Suite 911
Pasadena, CA 91439

Dear Mr. Keir:

Saying good-bye to a friend is never easy.

However, I have accepted a new position with another company. My last day of employment with CALIFORNIA COMMERCE WEEKLY will be Friday, January 15, 1995. My decision to leave CALIFORNIA COMMERCE WEEKLY is final.

I appreciate all that you have done for me in the past, and hope that we can maintain a cordial, professional relationship in the future.

Sincerely,

David Nelson

cc: Goodloe Suttler, VP Human Resources

8

Strengthen Your Candidates' Interview Performance

Candidate preparation is one of the cornerstone activities in our business. However, if you're like me, after about the five hundredth time telling a candidate to brush his teeth and comb his hair before an interview, you can get pretty tired of candidate prep.

To save time and avoid burnout, I make every possible effort to streamline my candidate preparation, and concentrate as much as possible on the qualitative issues surrounding the interview, rather than the generic techniques.

Interview Prep: Three Essential Elements

Before we focus our discussion on qualitative issues, let's review the three essential elements to interview preparation:

[1] *Logistics*. This involves the time, date and location of the interview, directions to the company (or off-site interview location), the names of the interviewers and their titles, appropriate phone numbers and so forth. Interview logistics also cover the interview time line and the administration of tests (personality, aptitude and drug screening); and if necessary, the details surrounding the company's location and candidate's relocation.

[2] *Protocol*. This involves the candidate's physical appearance, deportment, manners, interviewing demeanor, enthusiasm, and rapport building, probing and closing abilities.

[3] *Strategy*. This involves the candidate's knowledge or ability to determine from the interviewer important factors such as the company's direction, product focus, corporate culture, technical requirements, departmental problems, potential for growth, and so forth.

As you know, mastery of each of these elements is critical to interviewing success. For example, even the greatest candidate in the world won't stand a chance of getting an offer if he can't follow street directions or pass a drug test. And of course, what might be considered rudimentary for one candidate will appear as divine inspiration to the next.

It's our obligation to make sure the candidates we send out are as well briefed as possible in each of these areas. Logistics must be covered for every interview, as must strategy, since a candidate needs a compelling reason to interview with a company and have the means with which to get an offer.

However, it's in the review or teaching of the protocol, or interviewing basics, that many of us tend to spend most of our time; time that can to a greater or lesser degree be saved through the use of written materials.

A Refresher Course,
Not a Primer

Whenever a refresher course on the basics is called for, I simply give my candidates another of my *Career Development Reports* entitled "How to Master the Art of Interviewing" to read before their interviews. Since the written word has more staying power and authority than the spoken word, candidates retain and internalize more of the information than they would if I were to give them a pep talk five minutes before the interview, or the night before. By using the *Report*, I also avoid the risk of boring them to death or insulting them with my narrative, especially when I get to the part about wearing matching socks and removing their plastic pocket protectors.

Skipping the longwinded diatribe on the color of their tie or whether to wear Florsheims or Rockports helps reinforce my professional credibility, and allows me to concentrate on strategy issues, such as the specific needs of the employer, and how the candidate's unique skills will make a contribution.

Whether you're dealing with a highly polished talent pool or deserving candidates that need reinforcement of the basics, standardized written materials such as the Report can act as a valuable educational and time-saving tool. Not only will the information stay fresher in their minds (from reading it, not listening to it), they'll be more likely to conduct their interviews in a professional and thoughtful manner.

Six Keys to Interview Preparation

To adequately prepare a candidate for an interview, you should make certain that six key items are checklisted.

It's been said that Napoleon won his battles in his tent; that is, he did all the planning the night before the battle was joined, so that every contingency could be adequately covered. Interview preparation is similar. You and your candidate may never know exactly what will happen on the battlefield, but by being ready, you can eliminate a lot of the uncertainty, and your candidate will know how to react to different scenarios.

[1] The Resume

Your candidate should bring a couple of copies, and *read* his resume before the interview, so he's completely familiar with everything he's written. Nothing is more embarrassing (or potentially fatal) to your candidate than being quizzed on some aspect of his background that appears on the bottom of page two -- and not being able to remember the details.

Your candidate might also bring materials which might be particularly good at illustrating an important aspect of his work, such as creative designs, writing samples, and so forth. Discretion is, of course, the key.

I once interviewed an engineer who brought with him a lawn and garden string trimmer made by his current company, so he could show me the design improvements he'd made on the product. It turns out his engineering efforts had lowered the trimmer's cost to manufacture, which resulted in increased profits for his company. His version of "show and tell" was a bit extreme (my whole office was buzzing for weeks about my *weed wacker* candidate), but at least his real-life picture told me a thousand words.

Be careful, though, not to let your candidates overdo it with the props. College diplomas, letters of commendation, and company bowling trophies should be left at home. In nearly every interviewing situation, a resume and a business card are the most important props your candidate will ever need.

It's a good idea for your candidate to carry a leather folder or day runner with him so he can take notes or store written materials the company might hand him during the course of the interview. A briefcase is also fine, although a folder is lighter to carry, and less cumbersome.

[2] Appropriate Dress and Appearance

Much as I find some aspects of John Molloy's *New Dress for Success* (Warner Books, 1988) a bit disheartening, there's simply no practical excuse for a candidate dressing any way other than the book suggests. Sure, we'd all like to think that we're being judged on our qualifications, skills, and depth of character. But the truth is, when it comes to interviewing, in most cases, clothes make the man. To think any other way is to ignore reality.

Simply put, the more your candidate's appearance varies from the accepted norm, the less his or her chances of getting the job. This means that if your candidate's a male, he should wear a high quality gray or navy blue wool or wool blend suit, a white shirt, an understated tie, and black shoes, socks, and belt. If your candidate's a female, she should also wear a suit or business dress, and scale way back on the makeup, jewelry, and accessories.

For nearly every professional candidate, the general rule surrounding attire is: The more conservative, the better. Of course, there are exceptions. If your target industry is clothes conscious (as in retail, hospitality or entertainment), then there may be certain fashion statements that could be considered acceptable or preferred. But for the vast majority of occupations, when in doubt, play it safe.

While it's true that the candidate won't necessarily dress for work the way he'd dress for an interview, appearance is an important element in the interviewing protocol. You may not agree with the custom, but the choice is yours -- you can either go with the flow, or take your chances.

In *Take This Job and Leave It*, I told the story about a client company's corporate obsession with appearance, and how they knocked out a perfectly qualified candidate because he wore a beard.

It turns out I had another candidate scheduled to interview with the same company later in the week. This time, though, I wasn't going to make the mistake of sending him out without first checking to see what he looked like.

My plan was to pick him up at the airport and *hand deliver* him to the company. You can bet I wasn't about to have him show up wearing anything but the standard interviewing uniform. So the night before he flew into town, I called to give him explicit instructions on what to wear.

"Dave," I said, "I want to prepare you as well as I possibly can for your interview tomorrow. I'm going to get quite specific about your appearance, because it's important to the company, and may very well affect their decision to hire you."

"Okay, I can deal with that," said Dave.

"First of all, you're clean shaven, aren't you?"

"Yes."

"Good. Do you have a clean, navy blue pinstripe suit you can wear for your interview tomorrow?"

"Yes, I've got the suit."

"Fine. I want you to wear a white, cotton, button-down shirt. Do you have one?"

"Yes, I've got the shirt."

"Great. Now, do you have a dark red tie?"

"Yes, I've got the tie."

"Good. Can you wear black shoes, black socks, and a black belt?"

"No problem."

"All right. Do you need a haircut..."

"Wait a minute," Dave interrupted. "I think I know where all this is leading, and I want to assure you, everything's going to be fine."

"...You mean?"

"That's right, there's no need to worry," Dave said. "I vote Republican."

What I like about this story is that at the interview, the company fell in love with Dave, and hired him. I shudder to think what might have happened if he had dressed even a little bit differently (with brown shoes or a green tie, for example).

Admittedly, it's boring, having your candidates go to interviews dressed in a specific, premeditated uniform. But doing so takes all the guesswork out of what'll be successful and what won't. In a competitive job market, don't you want the odds on the side of your candidate?

[3] Travel, Arrival and Departure

A few years ago, a client company of mine flew a candidate to Los Angeles for an interview. The candidate, unfortunately, was unemployed at the time, and was in pretty dire financial straits. He charged the phone calls he made to his wife back in Wyoming and all his dry cleaning expenses (he only brought one shirt with him for two days of interviewing) to the company. Later, when the company received his expense voucher, they got pretty upset --- they never expected to pay for all these add-ons. It was too bad, too, because he was generally well received when he interviewed. I'd hate to think it was these little charges that were responsible for his not getting a job he really wanted; but each candidate has an obligation to act responsibly and professionally when dealing with an interviewing company.

Also, let your candidates know that the best time to arrive for an interview is precisely when they're scheduled, not early or late. It can irk an employer to be told that the candidate for a 2 o'clock appointment is waiting in the lobby at 1:35. The employer will either become distracted knowing there's someone hanging around waiting to see him, or he'll scramble to rearrange his schedule to accommodate the candidate, which disrupts the rest of his day.

Be sure to work out all the details regarding travel, arrival, departure, parking, directions, car rental, hotel check-in and so forth before sending your candidates out to meet their fate.

It'll put everyone at ease, and give the interview a higher probability of success.

[4] Name, Rank and Serial Number

The more information you can provide your candidate before an interview, the better. There are two reasons for this. First, you want him to be adequately prepared for the interview itself; and second, you want to avoid any surprises when he shows up for the interview. It can take a lot of wind out of the candidate's sails, for example, if he gets the impression he's going to meet the president of the company, and instead, spends 15 minutes interviewing with personnel.

When you arrange the interview, find out who the candidate will be talking to, and what their function is within the company. Candidates are only human, and will mentally prepare for a meeting with the CEO differently than with an internal recruiter or industrial psychologist.

I arrived exactly on time once for an interview with the general manager of a company I wanted to work for. I assumed that he and I were going to begin our interview right away. Boy, was I wrong. After greeting me in the lobby, he led me to a little office, where I was given two hours of intelligence, aptitude, and psychological tests. Had I not wanted the job so badly, I probably would have stormed out in a huff. True, he never told me I'd have to take any tests; but then again, I never asked.

[5] Digging Up the Dirt

While the amount of background information you can gather about a company is practically endless, it would be ludicrous to try to turn your candidate into a walking encyclopedia of corporate trivia. However, knowing something in each of these categories should significantly improve your candidate's odds of interviewing successfully:

- **The company's personnel** --- who the major

players are, who was recently hired or let go. It's also a good idea to know something of the history of the company, and who the founders were. For example, if you were interviewing for IBM, it might be considered a *faux pas* to look puzzled and ask, "Who?" at mention of the name Thomas Watson, Sr.

- **The company's basic structure** --- what products or services they provide to which customers, what the various divisions are, and whether they're privately or publicly held.

- **The company's vital signs** --- how the company is doing financially. Are they solvent or struggling? Are they involved in a hostile takeover, or merging with another company? How's their stock faring? You get the idea. Many of my candidates like to look through Value Line before they interview, so they can talk intelligently about the company's financial picture.

- **The company's corporate, divisional or departmental details** --- the changes that are taking place that could potentially affect the position you're interviewing for. Is there a new product introduction or marketing strategy in the works? Or how about an overhaul in the company's accounting methods, capital equipment, or computer system?

By arriving for their interviews adequately briefed, your candidates will make a strong impression on their interviewers. And best of all, they can spend their interviewing time discussing their background and how it matches the interviewer's needs, rather than the corporate biography or latest financial report.

[6] Candidates, Take Your Shopping List

During the course of an interview, your candidate's dialogue with the other person will spawn a number of questions spontaneously. However, there may be important issues to discuss that'll never come up unless the candidate takes the initiative.

For that reason, the candidate should bring a list of questions that will address these issues, so that he won't leave the interview uninformed.

Premeditated questions can be grouped into four different categories:

[1] *Company* questions deal with the organization, direction, policies, stability, growth, market share, and new products or services of the prospective company or department;

[2] *Industry* questions deal with the health, growth, change, technological advancement, and personnel of the industry as a whole;

[3] *Position* questions deal with the scope, responsibilities, travel, compensation policies, and reporting structure of the position he's interviewing for; and

[4] *Opportunity* questions deal with the candidate's potential for growth or advancement within the company or its divisions, and the likely timetable for promotion.

Your candidate may have specific interests or concerns surrounding topics in each category. For example, if he's interviewing with a computer manufacturer, he may want to ask about the future growth of the industry. Or, let's say he's interviewing for a position with a company that's known for its high rate of turnover. It might be helpful to prepare a carefully worded question that deals with that issue.

Don't Over-Hype Your Candidates

Whipping your candidates into a frenzy, filling them full of MBA babble, or infecting them with a near-fatal case of stage fright won't get them any closer to receiving a job offer. The truth is, the interview is only one of four factors affecting any hiring decision. The others are: past experience (the "resume"), test results, and references.

What this means is that a candidate can give a straightforward, functional interview and still be hired, based on the strength of one or more of the other factors.

Besides, a critical dimension of every hiring decision is out of their control anyway: the element of personal chemistry, or shared values. There's simply no way to rehearse for whether two people will like each other. And if you coach your candidates to fake the way they feel about the interviewer, they'll risk being exposed for fraud, or end up unhappy at the job. In either case, the whole purpose of referring them will be defeated.

There's no need to alter a candidate's identity for the sake of an interview. The best thing they can do is to relax, and rely on their empathy, common sense and forethought as the best means of preparation.

The Power of Empathy in Interviewing

Let's discuss empathy for a moment. In addition to its broad applications in selling, management and therapy, empathy can be used effectively any time you want to exchange ideas with another person. And when you think about it, that's exactly what an interview is: an exchange of ideas with another person.

Webster defines empathy as the "intellectual or emotional identification with another person's thoughts, feelings, or attitudes." So that begs the question: What are the thoughts, feelings, or attitudes of someone who's conducting an interview?

The answer is: You don't know, and neither does your candidate. Only by listening carefully and asking questions will the candidate find out the real needs of the interviewer. There's little point in your candidate selling himself unless he first learns what the interviewer is buying.

To a large degree, the success of your candidate's interview will depend on his ability to discover needs and empathize with the interviewer. He can do this by asking questions that verify his understanding of what the interviewer has just said, without editorializing or expressing an opinion. By establishing empathy in this manner, your candidate will be in a better position to freely exchange ideas, and demonstrate his suitability for the job.

The Information Exchange

In addition to empathy, there are four *intangible* fundamentals to a successful interview. These intangibles will influence the way your candidate's personality is perceived, and will affect the degree of rapport, or personal chemistry he'll share with the employer.

[1] *Enthusiasm.* Your candidate should leave no doubt as to his level of interest in the job, since employers often choose the more enthusiastic candidate in the case of a two-way tie. Besides, it's best for your candidate to keep his options open --- it's far better to be in a position to turn down an offer, rather than have a prospective job evaporate by giving a lethargic interview.

[2] *Technical interest.* Employers look for people who love what they do, and get excited by the prospect of getting into the nitty-gritty of the job.

[3] *Confidence.* No one likes a braggart, but the candidate who's sure of his or her abilities will almost certainly be more favorably received.

[4] *Intensity.* The last thing your candidate wants to do is come across as "flat" during the interview. There's nothing inherently wrong with being a laid-back person; but sleepwalkers rarely get hired.

Since interviewing also involves the exchange of *tangible* information, make sure your candidate:

- Presents his or her background in a thorough and accurate manner;

- Gathers data concerning the company, the industry, the position, and the specific opportunity;

- Links his or her abilities with the company's needs in the mind of the employer; and

- Builds a strong case for why the company should make the candidate an offer.

To ensure a successful interview, the candidate should never leave an interview without exchanging fundamental information with the employer. The more everyone knows about the other, the more potential you'll have for putting a deal together.

Understanding the Needs of the Interviewer

Besides reviewing the logistics and the basics of interviewing protocol, several general points of strategy should be shared with your candidate prior to his or her interview.

The first revolves around the candidate's ability to understand the needs of the interviewer. Unless the candidate asks high quality questions, the interview will quickly disintegrate into an interrogation or monologue. Candidate questions are the lifeblood of any successful interview, because they:

- Create dialogue, which will not only enable the two of them to learn more about each other, but will help them visualize what it'll be like working together once the candidate's been hired;

- Clarify the candidate's understanding of the company and the position responsibilities;

- Indicate the candidate's grasp of the fundamental issues surrounding the search;

- Display the candidate's ability to probe beyond the superficial; and

- Challenge the employer to reveal his or her own depth of knowledge, or commitment to the job and the company.

Candidate questions should always be slanted in such a way as to show interest, or an understanding of the employer's needs. After all, the reason for the sendout in the first place is that the employer's company has some piece of work that needs to be completed, or a problem that needs correcting. Here are some candidate questions that have proven to be very effective:

- *What's the most important issue facing your department?*

- *How can I help you accomplish this objective?*

- *How long has it been since you first identified this need?*

- *How long have you been trying to correct it?*

- *Have you tried using your present staff to get the job done? What was the result?*

- *What other means have you used? For example, have you brought in independent contractors, or temporary help, or employees borrowed from other departments? Or have you recently hired people who haven't worked out?*

- *Is there any particular skill or attitude you feel is critical to getting the job done?*

- *Is there a unique aspect of my background that you'd like to exploit in order to help accomplish your objectives?*

Questions like these will not only give your candidate a sense of the company's goals and priorities, they'll indicate to the interviewer his concern for satisfying the company's objectives. It's as if your candidate were writing a job order.

Try the Short Version First

The second point deals with the most common mistake inexperienced candidates make: the tendency to talk too much.

Remember, there are two ways to answer interview questions: the *short version* and *the long version*. When a question is open-ended, I always suggest to candidates that they say, "Let me give you the short version. If we need to explore some aspect of my answer more fully, I'd be happy to go into greater depth, and give you the long version."

The reason they should respond this way is that it's often difficult to know what type of answer each question will need.

A question like, "What was your most difficult assignment?" might take anywhere from 30 seconds to 30 minutes to answer, depending on the detail the candidate chooses to give.

Candidates sometimes need to be reminded that the interviewer is the one who asked the question. So the candidate should tailor his answer to what the interviewer needs to know, without a lot of extraneous rambling or superfluous explanation. In other words, why waste time and create a negative impression by giving a sermon when a short prayer would do just fine?

Let's suppose the candidate is interviewing for a sales management position, and the interviewer asks, "What sort of sales experience have you had in the past?"

Well, that's exactly the sort of question that can get a candidate into trouble if he doesn't use the short version/long version method. A poorly trained candidate would just start rattling off everything in memory that relates to his sales experience. Though the information might be useful to the interviewer, the answer could get pretty complicated and long-winded unless it's neatly packaged.

One way to answer the question might be, "I've held sales positions with three different consumer product companies over a nine-year period. Where would you like me to start?"

Or, the candidate might simply say, "Let me give you the short version first, and you can tell me where you want to go into more depth. I've had nine years experience in consumer product sales with three different companies, and held the titles of district, regional, and national sales manager. What aspect of my background would you like to concentrate on?"

By using this method, the candidate telegraphs to the interviewer that his thoughts are well-organized, and that he wants to understand the intent of the question before he travels too far in a direction neither he nor the interviewer wants to go.

After the candidate gets the green light to continue, he can spend his interviewing time discussing in detail the things that are important, not whatever happens to pop into his head.

The hiring manager of a food manufacturing company

once told me that he brought a candidate into his office to make him a job offer. An hour later, the candidate left. Did he end up hiring the candidate, I asked?

"No," he said. "I tried, but the candidate wouldn't stop talking long enough for me to make him an offer."

I'm not suggesting that an interview should consist of a series of monosyllabic grunts. It's just that nothing turns off an employer faster than a windbag candidate.

By using the short version/long version method to answer questions, your candidates will never talk themselves out of a job.

Money, Money, Money

There's a good chance your candidates will be asked about their current and expected level of compensation. Here's the way they should handle the following questions:

[1] What are you currently earning?

> *Answer:*   *"My compensation, including bonus, is in the high forties. I'm expecting my annual review next month, and that should put me in the low fifties."*

[2] What sort of money would you need in order to come to work for our company?

> *Answer:*   *"I feel that the opportunity is the most important issue, not salary. If we decide to work with each other, I'm sure you'll make me a fair offer."*

Notice the way a *range* was given as the answer to question [1], not a specific dollar figure. However, if the interviewer presses for an exact answer, then by all means, your candidate should be precise, in terms of salary, bonus, benefits, expected increase, and so forth.

In answer to question [2], if the interviewer tries to zero in on the candidate's expected compensation, he or she should also suggest a range, as in, "I would need something in the low- to mid-50s." Getting locked in to an exact figure may work against the candidate later, in one of two ways: either the number they give is lower than what they really want to accept; or the number appears too high or too low to the employer, and an offer never comes. By using a range, the candidate can keep his options open.

Avoiding the Fatal Mistake

Your candidate should also be aware that in first-level interviewing, there's one specific taboo in terms of the questions they ask: *Never, ever bring up the issue of salary or benefits*. If the employer initiates a dialogue surrounding these issues, and asks if they have any questions, fine.

But if it appears to the employer that the candidate's primary motivation for changing jobs is the new company's compensation or benefit package, the interview will screech to a grinding halt. Employers get chills when they suspect your candidate's only motivation for interviewing is to feather his own nest at the employer's expense.

Early in my recruiting career, I arranged an interview for a qualified candidate with a client company. After the interview, I called Shelly, the employer, to debrief her.

"Well, your candidate didn't do so well," Shelly said.

"Really? I thought he had the perfect background."

"That wasn't the problem. I just didn't like the way he handled the interview."

"What happened?"

"I spent over an hour with him, telling him everything about the company, and introducing him to all the key people," Shelly said. "I even gave him an extensive tour of the manufacturing area."

"And then?"

"And then, I brought him back to my office, and we sat down to talk about what he'd seen. I asked him if he had any questions."

"And did he?"

"Yes. That's when the interview ended. He looked me straight in the eye and asked, 'What are your benefits?'"

"And?"

"And I got up," Shelly said, "and walked him right out the door."

To be fair, the candidate's actions in no way reflected on his abilities or his character; his intentions were perfectly honorable. But after that incident (which cost the candidate a job and me a placement fee), I learned to caution interviewees not to initiate the subject of salary or benefits.

My suggestion is that candidates take the John F. Kennedy approach to interviewing: "Ask not what your company can do for you, ask what you can do for your company."

This way, the candidate can present himself as hard-working, virtuous, and dedicated, rather than as an opportunistic job-hopper who'd prefer to live off the fat of the land.

While it's unthinkable to accept or even consider a job without first knowing the financial rewards (or the details of the benefit package), there are better and more timely ways for you or your candidate to broach the subject, without endangering your candidate's chances (or your professional reputation).

No-Brain Questions and Candidate Contemplation

Here are seven of the most commonly asked interviewing questions. Do yourself and your candidate a favor, and ask the candidate to give them some thought before the interview occurs:

[1] Why do you want this job?

[2] Why do you want to leave your present company?

[3] Where do you see yourself in five years?

[4] What are your personal goals and interests?

[5] What are your strengths? Weaknesses?

[6] What do you like most about your current company?

[7] What do you like least about your current company?

The last question is probably the trickiest to answer: *What do you like least about your present company?*

I've found that rather than pointing out the faults of other people ("I can't stand the office politics," or, "I don't get along with my boss"), it's best for your candidate to place the burden on himself (as in, "I feel I'm ready to expand my capabilities," or, "The type of technology I'm interested in isn't available to me now").

By answering in this manner, your candidate will avoid pointing the finger at someone else, or coming across as a whiner or complainer. Besides, it does no good to speak negatively about others.

Suggest to your candidates that they think through the answers to the above questions. It won't help their chances any to hem and haw over fundamental issues. (Really, the answers to these questions should be *no-brainers.*)

But more importantly, the questions will help your candidate evaluate his career choices before the interview occurs. If the candidate doesn't feel comfortable with the answers he came up with, maybe the interview is a waste of time.

Four Questions You Can Count On

There are four types of questions that interviewers like to ask, and the better your candidate's prepared to handle them, the greater his or her chances of getting an offer.

[1] *Resume* questions relate to the candidate's past experience, skills, job responsibilities, education, upbringing, personal interests and so forth. Resume questions require accurate, objective, verifiable answers. The worst thing your candidate can do when tossed a resume question is to ramble on, exaggerate his achievements, or appear to be opinionated or egocentric.

[2] *Self-appraisal* questions require the candidate to make subjective comments on his abilities, or assess his past performance. Popular self-appraisal questions include, "What do you think is your greatest asset?" or, "Can you tell me something you've done that was very creative?"

[3] *Situational* questions explore the ways in which the candidate responds to different types of stimuli. A situational interview will focus on certain actions he took in the past, or require the candidate to explore hypothetical scenarios that may occur in the future. "How would you stay profitable during the next recession?" and, "How would you go about laying off 1300 employees?" and, "How did you handle customer complaints?" are typical situational questions.

[4] *Stress questions* test the candidate's mettle. Typical stress questions include, "After you die, what would you like your epitaph to read?" or, "If you were to compare yourself to any U.S. president,

who would it be?" or, "It's obvious your background makes you totally unqualified for this position. Why should we even waste our time talking?"

Stress questions are designed to evaluate a person's emotional reflexes, creativity, or attitudes while under pressure. Since off-the-wall or confrontational questions tend to jolt a person's equilibrium, or put him in a defensive posture, the best way for your candidate to handle them is to stay calm and give carefully considered answers.

Whenever I hear a stress question, I immediately think of the Miss Universe beauty pageant. The finalists (usually sheltered teenagers from places like Finland or Uruguay) are asked before a live television audience of three and a half billion people to give heartfelt and earnest responses to incongruous questions like, "What would you tell the leaders of all the countries on earth to do to promote world peace?"

Of course, your candidate's sense of humor will come in handy during the entire interviewing process, just so long as he doesn't go over the edge. I heard of a candidate once who, when asked to describe his ideal job, replied, "To have beautiful women rub my back with hot oil." Needless to say, he wasn't hired.

Even if it were possible to anticipate every interview question, memorizing dozens of stock answers would be impractical, to say the least. The best policy is for your candidate to review his background, priorities, and reasons for considering a new position; and to handle the interview as honestly as possible. If he doesn't know the answer to a question, it's best to just say so, or ask for a moment to think about a response.

Having the "magic answer" can actually work against you. One of my client companies declined to offer a candidate a job because he came up with a politically correct, prepackaged answer for every question they asked him. "Slick Nick" became the company's not-too-flattering nickname for an otherwise qualified candidate.

The Second-Level Interview

A *second-level* interview is much like the first, except that the list of questions from both sides will have become pretty well-focused. The second-level interview gives the candidate and the employer the chance to learn more about each other, and to delve more deeply into the details surrounding the position, the company, the industry, and the potential career opportunities within the organization.

In addition, both sides will be able to zero in on topics that were probably glossed over in the initial interview, such as the salary, benefits and relocation package.

If the interview is designed by the employer as an *offer interview*, then you and your candidate can begin to make the necessary preparations to put the deal together, address any loose ends, and set a tentative start date.

Long-Distance Interviews

The farther the distances separating the parties, the more complex the interviewing logistics become. Not only are travel and availability considerations difficult to deal with when scheduling, say, a Spokane-based candidate with a Tampa-based employer; such factors as weather and time zone differences can really play havoc with the interview. (Anyone who's ever tried to make a tight connecting flight in Chicago in February, or arrange a phone interview between Miami and Hong Kong will know what I mean.)

One technique I use to reduce the frustration of long-distance phone interviews is the *teleconferenced interview*. Invariably, employers "forget" to call candidates when they're supposed to, or candidates "forget" about the evening interview you've arranged, and fall asleep in front of the TV, only to be rudely awakened by an unforgiving employer. By scheduling the precise time and telephone locations, you can act as the master of ceremonies, and preside over an interview (or take the blame for any missed connections).

Teleconferencing the interview gives you the opportunity to listen in on the interview, and gain an insight into the dynamics and the flow of information from an objective perspective. If the employer has a concern over the way the candidate responded to a particular question, for example, you can offer your interpretation of what was said, and either soften the concern or disqualify the candidate, depending on the situation.

While teleconferencing can be viewed as an expensive and time-consuming proposition, in many cases it can cement a deal. My experience has shown that when used judiciously, the technique is one of the most cost-effective ways of gaining control over an often problematic situation.

Employer and Candidate Debriefing

Once the interview has occurred, it's vital that you get inside the heads of the employer and the candidate. As in any sales endeavor, it's impossible to assess where you stand unless or until you receive adequate feedback. By crafting a series of pertinent questions, you can address the following issues following an interview:

- **Clarity.** Did you accurately represent the needs of the employer? If the candidate's impression of position responsibilities was different than the way you described them, then you probably need to rework your understanding of the position.

- **Realism.** If the "fit" was good, what action will the candidate and the employer take? A lack of follow-up from either party may spell trouble, and may require you to reassess your position of strength or adjust your strategy relative to filling the position.

- **Control.** Information is power, and often, it can be

used to influence the outcome of your search assignment. For example, in cases in which a candidate is "almost, but not quite right" in the eyes of the employer, your intervention in the form of reference checking or bringing new information to light can make the difference between a deal and a bust.

It's sometimes helpful to look at an interview as more of a *process* than an event. Just because a candidate bombed during the first interview, you can't automatically assume the employer won't change his mind and hire the candidate.

Recruiters work best when they think like archeologists; by knowing how to interpret the hieroglyphic clues embedded in the decision-making process, your discoveries may lead to hidden treasure.

The better your candidates' preparation and debriefing, the better their chances of getting hired.

Fig. 8.1 An article will often attract candidates within your market niche.

GUEST EDITORIAL

What To Do When the Ax Falls

WILLIAM G. RADIN

Recently my organization launched a marketing campaign directed at companies in the $10 to $50 million range. To our surprise, 25% of the people we tried to contact were no longer at their jobs; they had either voluntarily or otherwise left their employers.

This fact underscores the pervasive nature of job liquidity. Your place of work may be the same a year from now, but with one out of every 14 people in the United States changing jobs yearly, you just might be confronted with a pink slip—or develop a sense of wanderlust—in the not-too-distant future.

If you do find yourself having to look for work, your best bet—unless you feel the time is right to change careers or start your own business—is to stick with what you know and improve the odds of landing a satisfying job. This can be done by strengthening your attack in three major areas: your resume, what I call your "coverage," and your interviewing skills.

YOUR RESUME

Your resume has to stand out in order to get the attention of decision makers. To strengthen its content and presentation, strive for improvement in these key areas:

Position title and job description. Provide your title, plus a detailed explanation of your daily activities and measurable results. Since job titles may be misleading, or their function may vary from one company to another, your resume should tell the reader exactly what you've done. (If you are a design engineer, what did you design?)

Detail. Specify some of the more difficult aspects of your work or education. Have you performed tasks of unusual complexity or significance? If so, don't be shy; give a one- or two-sentence description.

Dates and places. Don't leave the reader guessing where you were employed, or for how long. If you've had overlapping jobs, find a way to pull them apart on paper or omit one.

Relevance. Limit your material to that which is job related or clearly demonstrates a pattern of success. Concentrate on subject matter that addresses the employer's needs, not yours.

Explicitness. Leave nothing to the imagination. Don't assume the resume reader knows, for example, that your current employer supplies the fast-food industry with order-taker headsets.

Length. Keep it short. Writing more than two pages suggests that you can't organize your thoughts, or that you're trying too hard to make a good impression.

Spelling, grammar, and punctuation. Create an error-free document. Use a spell-check program, then check your work yourself. If you're unsure about your writing (or if English is your second language), consult a professional writer or editor. Always proofread what you've written.

Readability. Organize your thoughts in a clear, concise manner. No resume ever won a Nobel Prize for literature, but a poorly organized, unreadable, or shabbily prepared resume won't attract the kind of attention you want.

EXPAND YOUR COVERAGE

The positions listed in newspaper classified ads represent only a small fraction of the potential opportunities available to you, and rarely list all the engineering jobs available in a given geographical area.

Consider these other sources:

Electronic job listings, unlike classified ads, tend to be more highly descriptive of both the job and the hiring company. One such listing service, ADNET, advertises about a thousand current job openings, and serves nearly four million subscribers of networks like PRODIGY, CompuServe, Genie, and America Online.

Industry and professional journals, trade magazines, and newsletters often run help wanted ads, and furnish information that's of particular interest to their readership. The authors of technical articles are often employers themselves; you can call them directly to ask for help in your job search.

You'd be surprised at how many candidates I talk to have no idea of the number of companies (translation: potential job opportunities) in their industries. My experience has shown that for every company you already know about, there are at least two you never heard of that would benefit from your expertise.

SUCCESSFUL INTERVIEWS

The success of any job interview will depend on your ability to discern the employer's needs and empathize with the interviewer. Ask questions that verify your understanding of what the interviewer says to you, without expressing an opinion. Besides empathy, there are four other requirements for a successful interview:

Enthusiasm. Leave no doubt as to your interest in the job. Given a two-way tie, employers often choose the more enthusiastic candidate. Since employers look for people who love what they do, show your excitement for the nitty-gritty of the job.

Confidence. Nobody likes a braggart, but the candidate who's sure of his or her abilities will certainly be more favorably received.

Intensity. The last thing you want to do is come across as "flat" in your interview. There's nothing inherently wrong with being a laid-back person, but sleepwalkers rarely get employers excited. On the other hand, don't talk too much. Let the interviewer lead the way. Consider this: a manager I know brought a candidate into his office to make him a job offer. An hour later, the candidate left. Asked if he had hired the candidate, the manager replied, "No. I tried. But the candidate wouldn't stop talking long enough for me to make an offer."

Since interviewing involves the exchange of concrete information, present your background in a thorough and accurate manner. Gather data concerning the company, the industry, the position, and the specific opportunity and link your abilities with what you believe are the company's needs. Your goal should be to build a strong case for why the company should hire you, based on the discoveries you make from building a rapport with the interviewer and asking the right questions.

William G. Radin is president of Radin Associates, an executive search firm specializing in the sensor industry. The author of Take This Job and Leave It *and the forthcoming* Breakaway Careers, *he can be contacted at 2373 Brother Abdon Way, Santa Fe, NM 87505; 505-983-2243.*

9

Bolster Your Recruiting Power and Fill More Orders

Recruiting, like marketing, is a vital business activity that has the potential to generate big billings --- or completely waste your time.

It goes without saying that recruiting for bogus search assignments is a futile endeavor. By eliminating the time and energy spent serving the "needs" of unqualified employers and transferring your efforts to filling legitimate positions, you'll automatically increase your billings.

However, there are several techniques you can use to increase your overall efficiency when in hot pursuit of qualified candidates; and the implementation of any one of them should give you positive results, provided your client has realistic expectations.

Filing for Dollars

If you've been in the business for more than a few weeks, then you already know that the success of any recruiting effort will rest to a large degree on the functionality of your candidate filing and retrieval system.

Top-producing recruiters invariably have an orderly alpha or numeric system by which past and present candidates are accurately catalogued and cross-referenced. Whether or not you use a file drawer, a keyword-oriented resume retrieval system or an electronic database, the care with which you code your candidates (and the speed with which you can access their files) will greatly impact the efficiency of your search.

In addition to building a workable database of individual candidates, entire search assignments should also be catalogued for quick access. That way, once you've compiled a list of suitable candidates for a particular search, you can go back to the same list when a similar search rears its head at a later date.

Every time I execute a search, I keep a fairly detailed *search log* that's filed away for future reference should I ever need it. The search log is used mainly for reference and information retrieval, and includes names, dates and basic contact information (phone numbers, addresses and the like). The hard data that supports each search, such as resumes, debriefings, and company literature is filed separately.

With any luck, a six-month old search log will become the blueprint for an entirely new search, assuming the two searches share similarities in areas such as position, industry experience or skills.

The Quest for Synergistic Searches

If you were to need a different car to drive to every place

you went, your transportation expenses would really add up. Similarly, if you had to start every search totally from scratch, your time would be spent in a disproportionate state of preparation. That is, your production efforts would be focused more on the learning curve (where do I find them?) than on the qualifying of candidates (are they appropriate?). A different car for every destination, so to speak.

That's why your initial marketing efforts and your ability to prioritize your searches are so important. With a tightly defined candidate niche, you're less likely to dissipate your energy by trying to be all things to all people.

The most rewarding recruiting scenario is one in which one candidate can be presented to several different clients. Not only is your efficiency improved; so are your odds of making a placement.

EIOs Mean Efficiency and Control

The employer in office (EIO) strategy is a terrific way of improving your odds of filling a position. By batching your candidates together in a single interviewing session that lasts two or three hours, you not only save your client's valuable time, you also get to bundle your interview prep and debriefing chores.

EIOs are definitely the way to go, especially when recruiting in a local market. Additional advantages include:

- **Broadening the scope of acceptability.** An EIO allows you the latitude of presenting candidates that fall slightly above or below the employer's skill, experience or salary expectations.

- **Strengthening your professional credibility.** By conducting a smoothly running staffing center, you can prove your ability to take responsibility and capably administer your services.

- **Delivering what you promise.** An EIO also allows you to demonstrate your seriousness in helping satisfy the employer's staffing needs, by presenting a number of qualified candidates on a prearranged delivery date.

- **Participating in the hiring process.** You should always ask to sit in on the first 10 or 15 minutes of the initial interview. By so doing, you'll get a clearer picture of the open position, as well as an insight into the employer's interviewing style and line of questions (information, by the way, that you can share with the candidate who's next in line).

EIOs not only give you maximum control; they also allow you to use your referral creativity in a highly efficient setting.

Variations on a Theme

What's less known about EIOs is their adaptability to a variety of situations. For example, a technique that's worked well for me over the years is what I call the *multiple EIO*. Simply put, the multiple EIO is a staffing center set up in my office in which several qualified candidates are presented on a first-interview basis to not one, but multiple employers.

A variation on the multiple EIO is the *portable EIO*, in which your group of candidates interviews at one office with one employer, then packs up and moves to another location later in the day for a round of interviews with a second employer.

Back when I lived in Los Angeles, I turned a *remote* EIO (an EIO held at the employer's office) into a portable EIO with great success. After a morning round of interviews with a client at his plant location in the downtown area, my candidates got in their cars and drove to my Orange County office, where they interviewed with a second employer in the afternoon. Not only did I save a lot of time and energy setting up a total of ten different interviews (five candidates with two separate employers); I managed to set the stage for two placements on the same day!

Although they tend to work best on a local level, EIOs can be held in any location, and don't necessarily require that you be in attendance.

I lost a deal once to a sharp recruiter in Connecticut who scheduled an EIO in California with a client of mine from Ohio. My competitor had it all arranged via telephone, and by the time I found out about it, it was too late for me to do anything other than hope the other recruiter's candidates fell on their faces. Which they didn't --- one of them got the job, as a direct result of my competitor's remote EIO.

In *Billing Power*, I told the story of my former manager, who was able to hold an EIO in his car (no small feat, since the car was a Corvette) while he drove an employer to the Los Angeles International Airport. Not only was this an astoundingly innovative technique; it also proves the adaptability of the EIO as an effective means to put people together.

Knowing Where to Look

Just like the criminal who inevitably returns to the scene of his crime, your client will usually have an uncanny sense of where to find candidates. Your best source of referrals, in other words, is the hiring manager himself. If you fail to ask him to do a substantial part of the search work for you, you're just limiting your own efficiency.

Before I start a search, I make sure the employer fills out my executive search navigator, especially the portion that deals with past candidates, companies that are likely to produce candidates, and places that are potential sources of candidates, also known as *candidate breeding grounds*.

No advantage is too small when faced with a difficult search, and there's simply no reason not to ask for as much help as possible before you begin. Not only do I want to know the sources of all candidates interviewed to date, I also want to know where candidates with the requisite skills might be hiding, such as non-profit organizations, universities, research centers and so on.

It never pays to be shy when gathering useful information. On one search assignment, I asked the employer to run a computer printout of his company's direct competitors, complete with their addresses and phone numbers, and then circle the ones most likely to harbor suitable candidates.

On another assignment, I had the unmitigated gall to ask the HR manager from my client's competitor to send me all the resumes his company received from a recent ad for a similar position. To my amazement, 300 resumes arrived at my office via UPS the next day, and from the pile of unwanted candidates, I recruited one who was ultimately hired by my client.

I can't recall any special technique I used to solicit the resumes; I guess the HR manager was in a good mood the day I asked for them. But if I hadn't asked, I wouldn't have received.

Additional Sources of Referrals

There are a number of vehicles for increasing your candidate flow other than the investment of your personal phone time. These include:

- **Networks.** Many successful recruiters turn to all-purpose networks (such as National Personnel Associates) or niche market networks (such as the one I subscribe to, the *Recruiter News Digest* on the Internet) to augment their supply of candidates and increase their billings. However, unless you're relatively self-sufficient or really know how to work the network to your best advantage, you run the risk of becoming a network junkie, helpless without your weekly fix of resumes and split requests.

- **Collegial supporters.** By asking for help on a difficult search, you may find another recruiter who'll save the day by supplying you with the perfect candidate. Just remember, though, that even the most heartwarming split situation can turn sour if a post-placement problem arises that involves guarantees, minimum fees and the like.

- **Industry, trade and alumni directories.** Need I say more? These are the heart and soul of our research activities. Directories are not only worth their weight in gold, they can also be obtained for free if you know the right people or join the right association.

- **Company phone books.** Many companies publish in-house phone books for use by their employees. That recruiters might get their hands on these books and raid their people must have certainly occurred to them; otherwise, so many of the phone books wouldn't be coded.

- **Inter-company publications.** Most organizations of any size distribute monthly or quarterly newsletters to their employees. Chatty in nature, these publications read like a People magazine for recruiters --- in other words, all the movers, shakers, award winners and softball team captains you'd ever want to recruit are right there for the taking.

- **Patent ownership.** I like this technique. To locate brainy engineering talent, you can run a computer search of patent abstracts by subject, date and/or location at the library using the Cassis system. For every product on the market, there's an inventor (that is, a referral source or candidate) that's applied for patent protection.

- **Position advertising.** I've never placed my own ads for candidates; however, on rare occasions, I've written classified ads for my clients, who pay for the insertions. Naturally, on non-exclusive searches, you'll want to keep your clients' names confidential, and only give out your phone number, address or P.O. box.

- **Self-advertising.** Many recruiters run classified ads in trade magazines to increase their visibility and ultimately, their candidate flow. I've never run an ad, but doing so seems to work; otherwise, the recruiters running the ads wouldn't be investing their money.

- **Trade show attendance.** There's no fun like trolling for recruits. If you don't attend your target market's trade shows at least every other year, you're probably missing out on a wealth of opportunities.

- **Job fair participation.** You may not have the inclination to attend a job fair (many of them are generic or location-dependent and tend to attract unemployable or entry-level candidates). However, the job fair sponsors keep a fairly accurate list of attendees, and may make their names and/or resumes available to you.

- *The Directory of Executive Recruiters.* The most visible of all source books of recruiters, this directory is published annually by Kennedy Publications (Fitzwilliam, NH, 603-585-2200). I receive anywhere from five to ten unsolicited resumes a day as a result of my listing in the directory. Most of the resumes are totally inappropriate and end up in the trash; but someday, who knows?

- **Research assistance.** Your recruiting situation may require you to do all your own candidate sourcing, which is fine. On the other hand, if you're in a position to hire someone to help you, it might improve your overall efficiency. Lately, I've been using a former Korn/Ferry researcher based in Houston as a hired gun. For a list of independent researchers (whose fees range from $50 to $100 an hour), contact Ken Cole, publisher of *The Executive Search Research Directory* in Panama City Beach, FL, at 904-235-3733.

- **Personal visibility.** Whether you speak at your local Chamber meeting, write an article on changes in the work force, or attend a national trade association convention, your personal visibility will stimulate candidate referrals as well as marketing leads.

Naturally, each search situation will determine the usefulness of these various candidate flow vehicles. Whatever method you choose, remember that in our business, there's no such thing as too much high quality inventory.

Recruiting Scripts: General Principles Apply

If there were a single one-size-fits-all recruiting script guaranteed to snare the perfect candidate, I'd like to know about it, so I can retire right now.

As far as I'm aware, however, there's no such thing as a magic script. Each candidate will respond differently to every inquiry, depending on his motivation to make a change, or his generosity in referring an appropriate acquaintance.

That being said, there are four general principles of recruiting that I've found to be universal:

[1] *Candidates respond to benefits, not features.* Whatever you do, don't read your job order to a newly recruited candidate on your opening conversation. A recitation of the employer's wish list not only bores the candidate, it puts him off by making him feel like a replacement part, not a unique contributor. The best way to pitch your client's position is to describe it as a unique opportunity for the right individual, not a "job" that needs to be filled.

[2] *Candidates are intrigued by drama, not by the status quo.* That's why I always try to cast them in the role of problem-solvers or dragon slayers, rather than employment mercenaries working for a headhunting commander. A favorite script I use focuses on the predicament of an employer faced with the perils and promise of rapid growth; and through the help or interest of the recruited candidate, the good of many will be achieved.

[3] *Candidates should be approached indirectly for best results.* By asking "who do you know," the candidate functions in a potential double capacity: as a source of referrals, and as a possible recruit for your open position. By asking directly if the candidate is interested in the job, you run the risk of burning a set of leads, and scaring off the candidate by coming on too strong.

[4] *Candidates require varying amounts of romancing.* Whereas self-actualized candidates will get right to the point and read chapter and verse from their little black book within the first five minutes of

your call, less secure candidates will need a great deal of coaxing or rapport building before they'll trust you enough to reveal their innermost secrets.

Needless to say, patience and empathy can be tremendous virtues while in the act of recruiting. However, be careful not to let a prima donna lock you into an hour of meaningless chitchat; or worse yet, trick you into revealing information that's best left confidential, such as your client's identity. In other words, be selective in your rapport building; loose lips can definitely sink a search.

Multitasking and Long-Term Relations

In many cases, a candidate will fail to provide you with a lead or demonstrate a sincere interest in your search. However, he or she may still have value in the future, either as an employer, a candidate, or a referral source for subsequent searches.

Like a good reporter, it's in your best interest to develop a network of knowledgeable and talkative industry sources (known in the trade as bird dogs) that you can turn to in times of need. Your sources will not only benefit your business by referring candidates, spotting trends and alerting you to the hot employment gossip; they'll ultimately reap the rewards that come from being considered experts in their field. You might call it the law of karma.

Remember, for every person you recruit, you're developing a future source of industry knowledge and the competitive edge that you get from being well informed.

The more efficiently you recruit and develop relationships with candidates, the more often you'll fill your job orders.

Fig. 9.1 A search log will keep you focused, organized --- and profitable.

Radin Associates Search Log

Client Company _____ Position _____

Date	(✔)	Contact/Company	Remarks/Interview

10

Settle the Salary Disputes and Close More Deals

There's an age-old sales theory that "no" simply means the prospect lacks the information needed in order to say "yes."

If you're like me, and you subscribe to this theory, then it makes sense in any negotiation to keep supplying data until an agreement is reached and all options are explored --- especially when money is the issue in question.

As you know from experience, career-conscious individuals rarely make job choices based on money alone. Nonetheless, financial issues have the potential to trip up deals that are on otherwise solid footing.

While you might think that a candidate's indecision surrounding a fact-based issue like compensation would be relatively easy to resolve, just the opposite is the case.

Here's why: A person's compensation is an extremely quirky and subjective matter. The money a candidate earns not only affects his lifestyle (and that of his family), but also his self-esteem, self-identity and degree of upward mobility.

To make things more complicated, compensation can also be looked at from an objective viewpoint. Often, a negotiation over money seems like an encounter with a two-headed monster with a couple of 10-foot necks. Just when you think you've got one head under control, the other comes at you from a completely different direction.

Compensation Comparison: Just the Facts, Please

As recruiters, we have a responsibility to deal factually with our candidates' current and prospective income levels. Candidates depend on our due diligence with respect to financial matters, so they can make intelligent career decisions.

Therefore, we need to help them sort out the realities surrounding financial packages, in a manner that's efficient and easy to understand.

To begin with, we let them know that base salary is just the starting point when it comes to comparing the earning power tied to two different positions, especially if a relocation is required. To help a candidate objectively evaluate a job offer, several economic factors need to be considered. Here are some questions you need to ask the candidate about his current position before a salary decision can be reached:

- **Health and dental insurance.** How much is your company-paid insurance worth to you and your family each year? Do you pay a monthly contribution? If so, what's the amount?

- **Profit sharing.** How much did you receive in the form of distributions over the last year?

- **Pension plan.** Does your company offer a 401(k) plan? If so, how much is it worth to you as a tax shelter, and in terms of direct, company-paid contributions?

- **Retirement.** If you're not already vested, will you forfeit any money by leaving your present employer?

- **Life insurance.** Are you covered by your present company? How much would you have to pay to receive the same coverage?

- **Company-paid disability.** Are you covered? If so, for what amount? What's the premium worth to you on an annual basis?

- **Company car and/or gas credit card.** If these are a part of your package, how much are they worth to you per year?

- **Travel allowance.** Does your company pay you a fixed monthly sum?

- **Tuition reimbursement.** Is your company helping to further your education? If so, what's the dollar amount of their contribution?

- **Cash bonuses.** Are you being rewarded for a job well done? If so, what amount did you receive in the past 12 months?

- **Overtime or hazard pay.** What was it worth to you financially to risk life and limb last year?

- **Day care.** Do you work for a progressive company that provides this valuable service? If so, how much money did you save by taking advantage of it?

Once you've looked at the plus side of his current employment situation, you need to look at the negative, and ask the candidate what it's costing him to work at his current job. To keep score, see how your candidate responds to these expense related questions:

- **Commuting by private vehicle.** How much money do you spend to maintain, repair, and fuel your car, given your current commuting situation?

- **Toll charges.** Do you travel by turnpike or across a toll bridge to work? What does it cost you?

- **Parking.** How much do you have to pay to park your car where you now work?

- **Insurance.** Each state has different policies, regulations and characteristics that affect the cost of insurance. For example, I'm paying roughly 50 percent more in auto insurance in New Mexico than I paid in Ohio, due to the high ratio of uninsured motorists. Exactly how much are you paying for auto (or home or fire or earthquake) insurance where you now live?

- **Taxes.** Again, these expenses vary from state to state and from city to city. Consider for a moment (if you can do so without feeling sick) the various levies on your income, such as city, state, sales and property taxes. My brother, who lives in Ann Arbor, Michigan, pays roughly $7,000 a year in property taxes. If he were to move into a comparable neighborhood here in Santa Fe, his tax bill would be reduced by nearly $6,000.

- **Public transportation.** Do you commute by bus, rail, or rapid transit? How much do you spend a year?

- **Cost of living.** Do you live in an area with an inflated cost of living? If so, how much more are you paying in housing? In services? In utilities? In entertainment? In schooling for your children?

- **Long distance telephone charges.** Do you make business calls from home or on the road that aren't being reimbursed?

- **Tools of the trade.** Does your job require you to use a computer at home, or a modem, or a fax? What are you paying for the hardware, the software, and the supplies?

Remember that these variables work both ways. For example, your candidate may discover that a seemingly "low" offer from your client company actually represents an increase; while a "high" offer in a costly location may suffocate the candidate financially.

The Art of the Deal

A few years ago, I worked on behalf of a candidate who was earning $45,000 a year as a software engineer. The candidate was very reasonable in his salary expectations; as long as I could find him a new job that gave him the opportunity to develop his skills, he would be willing to accept a lateral offer.

Because he was already earning the reasonable and customary industry maximum for his level of experience, I asked him this question when we first discussed his salary needs: As long as I can get you $45,000 in first year total compensation, would that be acceptable to you? His answer was yes.

Two weeks later, one of my clients wanted to make him an offer. They'd interviewed him twice, checked his references, and felt certain he'd be a valuable asset to their company, a large, well-known manufacturer of machine tools.

But because of the prevailing salary structure within the company, they couldn't bring him on board for a penny more than $40,000 a year. Luckily, the employer, Art, was a pretty creative manager.

"Gee, Art," I said. "If only you could up the ante, I'm sure my candidate would accept your job offer."

"I'm really sorry," Art shrugged. "If we go any higher than $40,000, it'll upset the whole department, and I'll have a mass exodus on my hands."

"That could get ugly. But isn't there something we can do?"

"Let me give it some thought and I'll call you back. Will you be in your office later today?"

"Sure," I said, wondering what magic formula Art might have up his sleeve.

A couple of hours later, the phone rang. It was Art.

"Bill, didn't you tell me the candidate lived an hour outside the city?"

"That's right."

"Well, I'll tell you what. I'll throw in a gas credit card plus routine maintenance on his car. That would be worth about $1500 a year, right?"

"Sure, because he'd be commuting about 30,000 miles a year."

"And we can pay him overtime, at time and a half. If he works two extra hours a week at thirty dollars an hour, that's an extra $3000 a year. And we'll make it easy for him -- we'll loan him a PC and a modem so he can work overtime from home."

"That sounds great," I said. "But we're still five hundred dollars short."

"True, we are." Art paused. "Maybe we can't put this deal together after all."

"Wait a minute, I have an idea. His present company has a 401(k) plan, but it's non-contributory. What does your 401(k) plan provide?"

Art chuckled. "I think we found the answer. Our plan matches his contribution dollar for dollar up to $3000. All he'd have to do is contribute ten dollars a week, and he'd earn an extra $520 a year, tax-free. Do you think he'll accept our offer now?"

"We can give it the old college try," I said. "And thanks for finding a way to put this together."

Sure enough, the candidate accepted the offer, and was flattered that my client company thought enough of him to figure out a way to avoid making waves within the department.

New Angles and Crazy Placements

Most deals come together quite cleanly, with little need for haggling or creative financing. Sometimes, though, it takes a little imagination to satisfy both parties.

When a candidate's salary requirements exceed the published range for a position, or create an inequity within the department, then you've got a problem on your hands. In fact, these types of *salary equity* issues are the cause of most deals that fail to close for purely financial reasons.

To satisfy money matters, look for ways to increase your candidate's *overall yearly compensation*, rather than his or her *annual salary*. Here are a six types of goodies you can shoot for to boost your candidate's earnings without ruffling too many feathers:

[1] *A sign-on bonus* to be paid in cash on your date of start;

[2] *A performance bonus* to be paid after 30, 60 or 90 days, assuming the candidate's clearly defined goals are met;

[3] *A discretionary bonus* to be paid in a lump sum, or over a specified period of time;

[4] *A relocation bonus* to be paid on the candidate's date of start, ostensibly to cover closing costs and expenses (but which can be spent at his discretion);

[5] *An accelerated review*, which would occur after three or six months, rather than on the first anniversary of employment, after which the candidate's salary would be increased; or

[6] *An early participation* in the company's bonus, stock purchase, or pension plan; or other employee benefit program.

When required, companies will sometimes serve up these tasty morsels to hungry candidates who recognize that overall compensation consists of more than salary alone.

The craziest deal I ever put together involved a candidate who'd just purchased a home and was beyond commuting distance to the interested company. Since the candidate wouldn't sell his home and relocate, the company president agreed to buy the candidate (who had a pilot's license) a single engine airplane so he could *fly* to work each day. It just goes to show, where there's a will, there's a way.

What Would Ben Franklin Say?

Salary issues are seldom the only (or the most important) obstacles preventing a deal from closing. However, unless you can quantify the exact financial figures, you run the risk of causing buyer's remorse, when either the candidate or the employer learn the true value of the deal.

To avoid any surprises (or to support the hidden merits of

a seemingly low offer), I use a *position compensation comparison* to help the candidate place all the financial cards on the table in a straightforward manner. This one-page form is like a picture that tells a thousand words when it comes to illustrating the precise economic dimensions of a specific job offer.

For decisions that rest on subjective elements such as job satisfaction and the candidate's quality of life, I have the candidate fill out a form called the *position comparison guide*.

To a greater or lesser degree, each of these tools represents a disguised version of the oldest sales technique in the book, the Ben Franklin close.

The name of this close is derived from the way in which it's traditionally been pitched: the prospect is told to pretend he's the wisest man who ever lived, Ben Franklin.

As the legend goes, Ben would make an important decision by drawing a line down the middle of a blank sheet of paper and write the pros and cons in the appropriate column. The column with the higher score would then determine the outcome.

Whether or not Ben Franklin ever made decisions this way is anybody's guess. But as a practical (and time-saving) way to compare the relative merits of two different jobs, the comparisons work like a charm.

The Rules According to Freud

Most candidates have the intellectual acumen to point out the shortcomings of the position comparison guide, in which the decision is predicated on the equality of each point being considered. For reasons that should be obvious, a simple numerical tally of subjective issues has limited merits at best.

It should also be pointed out that you and I are in the business of making sales, and in any sales situation, the larger the deal becomes, the less logic plays a role.

I mention this because one of the great truisms that applies to the recruiting business can be attributed to Sigmund Freud, who once said that small decisions are based on logic, while large decisions are based on emotion.

Nonetheless, the position compensation comparison and the position comparison guide have been instrumental in closing deals over the years, because they help bring to the forefront the various factors that affect a candidate's decision to make a change.

The sooner you settle the salary disputes, the sooner you can close your deals.

Fig. 10.1 A compensation comparison will objectify the issue of money.

Position Compensation Comparison

Candidate _____ Current position _____

Old employer _____ New employer _____

Today's date _____ Start date _____

• Directions: Compare the position you have now with the one you are considering, according to the following elements:

Old job	New job	Element under consideration
$_____	$_____	Base salary
$_____	$_____	Bonus, perks
$_____	$_____	Profit sharing potential
$_____	$_____	Value of stock or equity
$_____	$_____	Pension (current value)
$_____	$_____	401(k) contribution, tax savings
$_____	$_____	Reimbursed expenses
$_____	$_____	Cost of living differential (+/-)
$_____	$_____	Non-reimbursed moving expenses
$_____	$_____	Job-related travel expenses
$_____	$_____	Insurance premiums
$_____	$_____	Property taxes
$_____	$_____	State taxes
$_____	$_____	Sales taxes
$_____	$_____	Other expenses (specify)
$_____	$_____	New job (+/-) $ _____

Fig. 10.2 A position comparison will shed light on underlying concerns.

Position Comparison Guide

Candidate _____

Old position _____ New position _____

• Directions: State your employment preferences according to the following elements:

Old job	New job	Element under consideration
[ ]	[ ]	Position title
[ ]	[ ]	Supervisory responsibility
[ ]	[ ]	Project authority
[ ]	[ ]	Decision-making autonomy
[ ]	[ ]	Freedom to implement ideas
[ ]	[ ]	Freedom to affect change
[ ]	[ ]	Promotion potential
[ ]	[ ]	Challenge of tasks
[ ]	[ ]	Ability to meet expectations
[ ]	[ ]	Access to skill training
[ ]	[ ]	Professional growth potential
[ ]	[ ]	Company/industry growth
[ ]	[ ]	Company/industry stability
[ ]	[ ]	Starting salary
[ ]	[ ]	Future compensation
[ ]	[ ]	Company benefits, perks
[ ]	[ ]	Commuting distance
[ ]	[ ]	Travel requirements
[ ]	[ ]	Working environment
[ ]	[ ]	Rapport with coworkers
[ ]	[ ]	Rapport with management
[ ]	[ ]	Comfort with corporate culture
[ ]	[ ]	Other considerations (specify)

Totals   _____   _____   New job differential (+/-) _____

11

Manage Your Time and Master Your Destiny

The principles of time management are fairly simple to master. The difficulty lies in maintaining the discipline to control your schedule, your tasks and your decisions as they relate to the efficient use of your only controllable commodity --- time.

I find it amusing whenever I see products that profess to manage your time through an organizational system of interchangeable flash cards, spiral-bound planners or elaborate computer programs. These tools may be fine for organizing your papers or reminding you of appointments, but they have relatively little to do with the fundamental laws of proper time management.

Face it, if an activity is essentially useless, it makes no difference when or where you do it, it's still a waste of time. Successful people, whether they're recruiters or steel workers or homemakers, don't work twice the number of hours to achieve twice the results. They work smarter by eliminating from their lives the activities that waste their time.

The Process of Elimination

It's no secret that the choices we make in life often determine our happiness, or our success.

In the business world, the more often you take actions that are beneficial and sidestep those that are detrimental, the more likely you'll be to achieve your goals. Recruiting, in a sense, is largely a matter of making executive-level decisions with respect to a number of key areas:

- **Market.** A poor choice of constituency can put you in the penalty box. For example, I know the owner of a perm clerical agency who can't compete in her regional market against temp agencies that specialize in temp-to-perm conversions. No matter how many extra hours the owner might be willing to work, the fact that she's swimming against the prevailing business current remains unchanged.

- **Clients.** Sadly, we sometimes get locked into dysfunctional relationships with lousy clients who mistreat us in a myriad of ways, subtle and otherwise. Once you start to believe that your survival depends on a certain client, you've fallen into the business equivalent of a "battered spouse" syndrome. As painful as it might be to make the break, you'll be surprised how well you'll do without an abusive client chained to your ankle.

- **Candidates.** Have you ever fallen in love with a

candidate (not literally), and continued to work with him long after his usefulness had expired? I have, and my affairs have cost me dearly. If a candidate fails to generate interest with your clients after several attempts, put him in your *deep freeze* file and stop wasting your time trying to place him.

• **Job orders.** If I'm on the phone with an employer and we're discussing a position that sounds impossible to fill, I won't even bother writing a job order or sending a proposal. I'll advise the employer to call every recruiter he knows and let him waste their time. If I have a resume in my files that fits the bill, fine. But I won't spend a lot of time looking for it, and I certainly won't spin my wheels networking or flash recruiting. I'll invest my time on activities with a more likely return.

• **Searches.** As they used to say on *Hill Street Blues*, let's be careful out there. No matter how hard you want to please a client or earn a fee, some searches are going to be more trouble than they're worth, and if you let them, they'll sit on your shoulders like a 200-pound gorilla.

Once I get a sense that an employer will only settle for the holy grail, I'll grind my good faith crusade to a halt and move on to greener pastures; or farm out the search to another recruiter and pray for a split.

Twelve Ways to Save Your Time

In our business, time management can be defined as common sense mixed with a healthy skepticism. To avoid costly expenditures of time and energy, here are twelve additional time management techniques:

[1]   *Prioritize your tasks.* Since all activities are not created equal, your energies will be best spent doing the things that carry the most weight in terms of immediate results.

[2]   *Delay the unnecessary.* Often, a low-priority call or meeting can be put off until a later date, or canceled altogether. If a meeting is really important, you'll find the time for it. If it's not important, then why bother with it at all?

[3]   *Manage your relationships concisely.* Without a doubt, routine service calls and follow-up calls are vital in a people-oriented business. Just make sure these types of calls don't take precedence over more pressing activities, and be sure to keep your calls short and to the point.

[4]   *Batch your tasks.* If you're making marketing calls, put several of them in front of you and hammer away. In other words, don't mix your activities; focus on a bite-sized series of nearly identical tasks until they're completed.

[5]   *Avoid the temptation to oversell.* In our business, it's easy to cross over the line from being persistent to being obnoxious. It makes much better business sense to tickle your prospects occasionally than to suffocate them regularly.

[6]   *Forget the missionary work.* Some people you sell to just won't "get it," no matter how skillfully you try to persuade them. When dealing with resistant prospects, I remind myself of the old adage, "Never try to teach a pig to sing. It just wastes your time and annoys the pig."

[7]   *Economize whenever possible.* Look for shortcuts

that might spare you the need to reinvent the wheel, such as holding multiple EIOs, standardizing your internal paperwork, resurrecting candidates from previous searches and reworking the same letter or marketing communications piece for different applications.

[8]   *Shorten your calls and meetings.* Most of us like to chat on the phone; maybe that's why we chose recruiting as a profession. Just remember that while quality is an important issue, most calls or meetings can be just as productive in five minutes as they can be in fifty. Gotta go.

[9]   *Pick your spots on the playing field wisely.* For every client visit that's a success, two or three are a total waste of time. If you can't prepare a concise, goal-oriented agenda prior to a client visit, don't go at all.

[10] *Transfer your workload to someone else, not vice versa.* In the case of splits, for example, I'll gladly ask another recruiter for assistance in finding a candidate, but will rarely assume the role of researcher for someone else's job order. Unless your business is designed as a cooperative, in which all tasks are shared, it's best to decline the job of "helper."

[11] *Politely duck the walk-ins and call-ins.* Does your doctor see you without an appointment? Mine doesn't. Similarly, I regulate my time to protect myself from unsolicited people seeking my help. If I do decide to see someone, it'll be on my time management terms, not theirs.

[12] *Work within your lifestyle, business cycle and physical idiosyncrasies.* Long ago, I began to limit the

number of evening and weekend calls I made, and it hasn't hurt my production one iota. In addition, I try to perform tasks that are in sync with my biorhythms (I hate that term, but I can't think of a better one). For example, like many people, I'm at my most creative in the morning, so that's when I write letters and work on new marketing ideas. Tasks that can be done by rote are reserved for the afternoon; and I pay special attention to time-sensitive issues such as client work schedules, time zone differences and postal delivery deadlines.

At first, my biggest fear about time management was that in order to be efficient, I would have to transform myself into some sort of soulless robot, resigned to life in a mechanized purgatory similar to Charlie Chaplin's in the movie *Modern Times*.

Fortunately, I came to realize that time management is simply a tool with enormous power to make life easier. To become a robot would actually violate time management's fundamental premise: that *you* can control the use of your time, not vice versa.

What You Want is a Balanced Life

By far the greatest benefit to time management is that it gives you the means to live a balanced life, by replacing the time you waste with the time to enjoy outside interests.

There's no way to avoid the long hours and intrusions into your privacy that are part and parcel with being a successful recruiter, especially within the first few years of getting into the business.

However, with careful time management and deliberate control of your business, you can eliminate much of the stress and fatigue that eat away at your ability to function at a peak level. And as long as you keep making strides in your professional abilities, your billings will increase naturally.

In terms of goal setting, lest you make yourself crazy, I suggest you adjust your goals so they're congruent with your self-image and fundamental values, and compete most fervently with yourself, not others.

As long as you keep developing according to the goals that are important to you, your business associates, and those you care about, everything will turn out just fine.

The efficient use of time will boost your earnings and improve your quality of life.

12

Retro-Market Your Service to Long-Lost Customers

It's only natural to concentrate your business development activities on brand new clients.

By doing so, however, you could be overlooking a fertile source of revenue --- long lost customers.

Long lost customers aren't just the clients you worked with ten years ago; they're also the "warm" prospects who are in some way prequalified and positioned to make use of your services.

Long lost customers often make for perfectly viable prospects who are eminently worthy of your retro-marketing efforts. These customers include:

- **Past employers who have paid you a fee.** If you made one placement with a company, then it stands to reason you can make another.

- **Unrequited employers.** These are hiring managers who have given you search assignments that for one reason or another were never consummated.

- **Current employers who may have additional needs.** Most companies of any size usually have more than one open requisition at a time; and it's your job to help them fill all their needs, so long as the needs fall within your area of expertise and competency.

- **Related employers.** Many companies have familial divisions. If you can figure out a way to work up, down or laterally within a big enough corporation, you could keep yourself busy for a lifetime.

- **Disinterested employers.** Let's say your proposals have ended up in the trash for the last two years. Because situations (and a company's personnel) change, you can't automatically assume that you'll never make a sale.

- **Dissatisfied employers.** Well, nobody's perfect. But that doesn't mean that you can't rebuild a good relationship with a company or individual with which you've experienced friction.

- **Deadbeat employers.** Collection calls, if they're handled in a service-oriented manner, can sometimes result in repeat business.

Interestingly enough, I've found that most companies that are slow to pay have good intentions. So if you can live with a drawn out payment cycle (or cajole your client into more expeditious behavior in the future), you may be able to turn an enemy into a friend.

Service Calls and Questionnaires

Over the last few years, concepts such as "total customer satisfaction" and "total quality management" have been all the rage.

Business school theories, however, are strikingly different from reality; and until you can accurately measure the results of your quality control and customer satisfaction efforts, you'll never know exactly where you stand.

To quantify your business relationships, it makes good sense to design a questionnaire and poll your customers as to their feelings about your service.

A well-written questionnaire that's administered by an objective third party will give you a fairly accurate insight into the way you're perceived in the market, since it will allow the customer to speak freely, without the possibility of hurting your feelings.

Third party inquiries also put the customer at ease, because third parties have nothing to gain from the conversation, and don't sound like salespeople who might be using the "customer survey" format as a thinly veiled ruse.

The surveys for Radin Associates are conducted by a market research firm in Indiana that specializes in political and business research. The firm not only helps me refine the questions, they also execute the survey and track the results. Their fee of $13 a response is, to put it mildly, well worth the investment.

Unless your survey consists of a very informal discussion with a client (as in, "Well, how'd I do?"), you should poll as many people as possible. That way, you can minimize the chances of your results being skewed from the lack of a large enough sample.

Until you have a minimum of 25 respondents, your results will probably lack sufficient validity to warrant substantial changes in the way you do business.

Lost Customer Surveys

Whenever I market my business via direct mail, it's a given that the response rate will remain at a constant two percent; that's a number that's out of my control.

What I can control (or at least improve) is my closure ratio. To explore for the reasons behind a customer's refusal to buy, I make use of a *lost customer survey* that asks respondents to rate my service in several different areas.

I believe that any time you can focus on the precise elements that impact your customer's willingness to buy, then the feedback you get from them will allow you to make adjustments that will produce a more favorable outcome.

If you can get your business to hit on all cylinders, you'll not only improve your horsepower, you'll stop worrying about weaknesses that exist only in your imagination.

I ran a survey once because I theorized that either my initial telephone presentation or my marketing materials were restricting my closing ratio.

What I found as a result of the survey was that with respect to these two areas of concern, I received the highest ratings. Instead, my customers' concerns dealt more with the perception of my terms and conditions than anything else.

Armed with this vital market information, I then made the necessary adjustments to minimize these concerns, and as a result, my business improved.

Questions Designed for Maximum Effect

The way in which you script the questions you ask in a satisfaction survey is just as critical as the way you might script a cold call or marketing presentation. For maximum effect, it's best to use a combination of quantitative, qualitative and open-ended questions.

For example, a yes-no question such as "Would you ever use a service such as ours?" has little value, in that it fails to expose the underlying concern if the answer is no.

Instead, I would reshape it into a question like, "Under what circumstances would you use a service such as ours?" or, "On a scale of one to ten, how likely is it that you would hire Radin Associates within the next six months?"

In terms of the elements you want to survey, you might as well cover as many bases as possible. These could include:

- **Price.** How do you compare with the competition? Are you disproportionately high or low relative to the services you provide?

- **Terms.** Are your guarantees (real or imagined) or payment terms keeping your customers away? If so, what can you do to bring them into the fold?

- **Value.** Do you offer a solution or insight that your competitors don't; or bring about a result that clearly can't be realized from within the organization?

- **Interpersonal qualities.** Are you perceived as being knowledgeable, trustworthy, competent, responsive and professional? If not, what did you say or do in the past that might have turned the customer off?

- **Communications materials.** Are your brochures, letters, fee agreements and contracts clearly written and representative of a first-rate organization?

Don't overlook the inclusion of questions that might identify an unqualified prospect or otherwise invalidate your survey. If, for example, the questionnaire reveals that the customer laid off 90 percent of its work force, filed for bankruptcy or filled the last ten positions from within, then you know that nothing you could have said or done would have made any difference.

The Power of Self-Evaluation

As beneficial as it is to query your customers, it also makes sense to evaluate your own recent victories and setbacks. By analyzing what you did right or wrong, you can emphasize the positive aspects of your work in the future and make changes to counterbalance your mistakes.

One of the best tools for self-evaluation is a form I call the *anatomy of a placement* (or *autopsy of a placement*, depending on the outcome of the search). This survey is not only useful in scrutinizing past events, it also helps me make objective decisions whenever I'm faced with the decision of whether or not to drop an existing client.

As you know, not all clients are created equal. Each will vary to some degree, not only in terms of temperament and style, but in structural characteristics.

For example, even if you and a decision-maker get along on a personal basis, there may be inherent obstacles that will prevent you from giving your best service, such as company policies regarding interviewing, hiring or paying for consulting services.

The *anatomy of a placement* is designed to quantify many of the key issues surrounding your business relationships. Once these issues are understood, you can decide what direction to take with respect to each of your clients.

By taking stock of your entire customer base, past, present and future, you can more efficiently serve the needs of your market. For all the time we spend trying to develop entirely new business (or cling to codependent client relationships), it's nice to know that success can be lurking right under our noses.

**Long lost customers often represent
the key to increased billings.**

Fig. 12.1 By interviewing lost customers, you can improve your service.

Lost Customer Survey

Company _____

Hiring manager or contact _____ Title _____

Date of initial inquiry or response _____ Today's date _____

1. Earlier this year, we discussed a search for (position) _____

   Did you ever find the individual you were looking for? Yes _____ No _____

2. If yes, how did you find him? (Was it through a competitive service?)

   (If so, why did you choose them to conduct the search?)

   (How is the person you found working out?)

3. If no, how do you plan on finding the right candidate?

4. Why did you decide not to use Radin Associates' services? Was it price?

   Lack of industry or technical expertise?

   Inability to understand your needs?

   Lack of confidence in their ability to produce results? Other?

5. In regards to Radin Associates' service, how would you improve:

   The telephone presentation made by Bill Radin when you called him?

   The support materials we sent (company literature, folder, etc.)?

6. Could you suggest any ways in which we could improve our service?

7. Would you be interested in using Radin Associates' services in the future?

   If yes, when should we contact you?

   If no, is there anything we could change that would make you reconsider?

8. Are there any other departments that might benefit from our service at this time?

9. One last question: Should we keep you posted in terms of career opportunities?

Fig. 12.2 This survey helps correlate recruiting activity with results.

Anatomy (or Autopsy) of a Placement

Client company _____

Hiring manager _____ Title _____

Assignment date _____ Conclusion date _____ Today's date _____

Number of hours (days, weeks) worked _____ Placement? _____ Yes _____ No

• Directions: Rate the following elements of your placement, job order or search
            disaster from weakest (1) to strongest (5).

1. Overall knowledge of the client company	1 2 3 4 5
2. Knowledge of the position qualifications and responsibilities	1 2 3 4 5
3. Amount of quality time spent discussing hiring manager's needs	1 2 3 4 5
4. Amount of quality time spent in direct contact with hiring manager	1 2 3 4 5
5. Company's true urgency in filling the position	1 2 3 4 5
6. Flexibility of the decision-maker to widen the qualifications	1 2 3 4 5
7. Attractiveness of the client company to potential candidates	1 2 3 4 5
8. Competitiveness of the compensation and/or benefit package	1 2 3 4 5
9. Turnaround time from candidate introduction to interview	1 2 3 4 5
10. Turnaround time from interview to offer	1 2 3 4 5
11. Autonomy of your contact to make or expedite a hiring decision	1 2 3 4 5
12. Rapport between the recruiter and the hiring manager	1 2 3 4 5
13. Availability and "recruitability" of qualified candidates	1 2 3 4 5
14. Fairness of your fee agreement with the client company	1 2 3 4 5
15. Candidate crossover potential to other search assignments	1 2 3 4 5
16. Degree to which the position is in your target market	1 2 3 4 5
17. The potential for doing repeat business with this client	1 2 3 4 5
18. Other factor or factors (specify)	1 2 3 4 5

• Total score   _____

Grade: 75-90 Extremely strong • 60-74 Strong • 45-59 Weak • Under 45 Extremely weak

Areas of strength _____ Areas that need improvement _____

13

Write Your Business All the Way to the Bank

In some circumstances, the exclusive use of the telephone can limit your market penetration, since [1] you can only make so many calls a day; and [2] not every prospect can be reached via the phone, no matter how skilled you are at breaking through the barriers set up to screen you.

Simply put, there are going to be times when cold calling will be ineffective or even counterproductive. This is especially true when dealing with people who've built up an immunity from fielding annoying telemarketing calls from people such as stockbrokers, timeshare peddlers and credit card purveyors.

An Effective Alternative

To extend my reach as far as possible with "phone resistant" prospects, I've found that an extremely effective alternative to telephone cold calling is direct mail marketing.

Like cold calling, direct mail marketing is the art and science of sending a standardized message to a large number of prospects with the goal of generating interest that will directly or indirectly lead to a sale.

Whether or not you decide to actually use direct mail as a marketing tool, I urge you to learn as much as you can about the principles of direct mail, because in many ways they parallel the fundamentals of cold calling. In other words, the more you know about one strategy, the more you'll know about the other.

The Two Percent Solution

If executed properly, a direct mail campaign will yield a two to three percent return. While this might not sound very exciting, you have to remember that there are a number of key advantages to direct mail that counterbalance the relatively low return rate. These include:

- **Firepower.** Your message can reach 5000 prospects next Wednesday. Can any single telephone cold caller make that claim?

- **Standardization.** The essential message you send is always the same, and gets repeated every time you reach the prospect (message standardization, as in, *it's the economy, stupid,* helped get Bill Clinton elected).

- **Message uniformity.** A letter never has mood swings, never varies in its basic appeal, and never needs to rely on intangibles such as "chemistry" or "rapport" with the prospect for success.

- **Lateral coverage.** The direct mail piece you send can be shared by several people or photocopied for general consumption.

- **Staying power.** Your letter or brochure can be filed away and referred to at a later date. It may even outlast the person it was originally sent to, and be found and acted on by a successor.

- **User friendliness.** Unlike a phone call, a letter never interrupts a meeting or makes the prospect late for an appointment. A prospect can choose the right time to mull over your message, whether it's at the office, at home, on a flight or in the executive washroom.

Direct mail marketing makes a lot of sense in a business that's essentially a numbers game (like ours), since it allows you to throw a huge net over many more prospects than you can realistically reach by phone.

Message Delivery *en Masse*

From a purely practical standpoint, direct mail marketing provides an efficient, cost-effective vehicle for mass message delivery. Some of the benefits include:

- **Regularity of delivery.** Your mailings can keep to a rigid schedule, regardless of how busy you are doing other things.

- **Cost control.** Direct mail expenses can be predicted, budgeted, adjusted and tracked over time.

- **Time management sensitivity.** Printing letters and stuffing envelopes can be done by a support staff, a temp, or in the evening hours, thus freeing up your work day for more important activities.

- **Minimal investment per "hit."** If the prospect has no interest and throws away your letter, you've spent less money than you would making a long distance phone call, and wasted absolutely no selling time.

This last point is important when you compare the relative merits of direct mail versus cold calling. Assuming you're going to "waste" a large percentage of your message on hundreds of indifferent prospects, it's more cost-effective to do it in the format of a letter than a phone call.

What's more, a cold call can waste your time or even work against you if you're having a bad day and you're trying desperately to "sell" to a congenitally sales-resistant prospect.

Or to put it another way, if your letter ends up in the trash, how much have you really lost?

The List, the Piece and the Offer

The principles of direct mail marketing are fairly simple, and are surprisingly similar to cold calling. In essence, the success of any direct mail campaign depends on three basic factors:

[1] *The list*, or target market;

[2] *The piece*, or the message you send and the way it's put together; and

[3] *The offer*, or the nature of service you provide, and the way it's perceived by the prospect, in terms of benefits and affordability.

The people who use direct mail value their list above all else, and for good reason. Without a strong list, your campaign will be all dressed up with no place to go.

Growing and maintaining a list is like growing and maintaining a field of sweet corn. With a little bit of seeding, feeding and weeding, you'll harvest a crop of perpetual profits.

However, no matter how strong your list may be, if your piece is weak, so will be your response. By the same token, a beautifully designed piece will languish if your offer is lacking in perceived value.

Direct Mail Versus Junk Mail

Before you can build a list, you need to study the demographics of your "ideal customer," and how these customers are most effectively reached via the U.S. Postal Service. It's worth noting that what distinguishes direct mail from "junk mail" is the accuracy with which an appropriate piece is targeted.

For example, when an L.L. Bean catalog is delivered to a Mr. Al Gore in Washington, D.C., identified by a demographic survey to be a well-educated, upscale baby-boomer who travels frequently and owns a Jeep Cherokee, then that's direct mail marketing at its finest.

But when the same catalog is sent to "occupant" at the Pia Zadora Golden Buckeye Retirement Village, then we're talking junk mail, since the piece and the offer are out of sync with the recipient on the list.

To build a list, you should start with your precise industry constituency, including your past contacts, plus names gleaned from industry directories, trade magazines, buyer's guides, business weeklies and so forth.

Your specific target market will depend on your desk specialty, and can be further defined by each target company's location, products, talent pool, size or other combination of characteristics. For a general mailing, a simple Standard Industrial Classification (SIC) designation might suffice; for a surgical strike, you'll need to target a very specific constituency in order to be most effective.

The prospect's name, title, company name, address (and phone number for future reference) will then need to be entered into your database. I happen to use a Macintosh-compatible relational database with word processing and mail-merge capabilities called SOLO™, developed by mega-recruiter and computer ace Bill Vick of Plano, Texas. (Call Bill at 214-612-8425 for more information.)

For direct marketing purposes, you should only gather the basic information you need about a prospective customer; it's a waste of time to thoroughly research each company. The objective, after all, is simple target marketing with an expected failure rate of 98 percent. Direct mail information overkill will do you about as much good as dropping a fax machine in the middle of the Sahara.

Adding to the List

If you don't have the means to build a list for yourself, or you want to supplement the list you already have, you can rent a list from an independent list broker who either specializes in certain fields or compiles data from public sources such as the yellow pages or industry directories like Standard & Poors or Dun & Bradstreet. Usually, you'll have a choice of receiving mailing labels arranged the way you want, either alphabetically or by zip code; in some cases, lists are available on-line or on floppy disk or CD-ROM formats. If you buy labels, don't try to cheat the list seller by copying the list for later use. Lists are usually "seeded" with phony or coded contacts that can be easily traced back to the sender, and you'll get caught.

To supplement my custom-built list, I've entered into a licensing agreement with a company called MarketPlace Business of Cambridge, Massachusetts. They supply me with a CD that provides data on nearly 10 million companies nationwide, updated on a quarterly basis. The list is quickly searchable, either by name, geographic location, phone number, size of company (number of employees or annual sales) or eight-digit SIC code. With this degree of specificity, I can create a mailing list of companies in Arkansas that manufacture at least $5 million worth of automotive gaskets annually. MarketPlace can be reached at 617-672-9220.

Another option is to trade lists with other direct mailers, or barter for lists. For example, I recently obtained an alphabetized list of the 1,500 corporate subscribers of a technical magazine in exchange for a two-part editorial the magazine asked me to write.

Yet another alternative is to skip the brokers and work directly with list publishers, such as the phone company, the Chamber of Commerce or the publishers of industrial or trade directories. Trade magazines and newsletters will also offer their subscription lists to direct mailers for a fee, which varies according to the list's size, the number of times you wish to use the list and the quality of the prospects.

List Inequality

When it comes to direct mail, all lists are not created equal. Not surprisingly, a list containing the name of the president of each company will cost more to rent or purchase than a list of companies addressed to a generic title.

The most valuable lists are, in decreasing order, the ones that contain the names of:

- **Past customers,** especially those you've worked with recently;

- **Qualified prospects,** who are prospects known (or suspected) for their potential to want your service; and

- **Generic prospects,** who may or may not be interested in what you have to offer.

Lists are perishable, and like baseball cards, will vary considerably in their worth with respect to the knowledge of the collector.

Just remember that quality will often counterbalance size; however, with a two percent return, there's no substitute for quantity.

Target the Top of the Food Chain

For maximum efficiency, I send one letter per company. In my first few mailings, I sent as many as ten letters to different people within the same company, but found that my return rate was lower than the one-to-one ratio I now use. And although I work a sales and marketing desk, I've learned from experience to target the company president, not the sales manager.

By targeting the top of the food chain, I automatically pre-sell the highest level decision-maker. So when the president hands my letter to the sales manager, there's already a *de facto* consensus that the search is needed, and my service has gained tentative approval from the top. This, of course, is similar to the strategy you or I would use when cold calling.

Less effective are letters addressed to vague entities such as "general manager" or "MIS Director." Letters like these are generally sniffed out as direct mailer letters, and are less likely to be taken seriously (or even opened) than letters written to specific individuals by name.

Consistency and Repetition

Another few points are worth mentioning. First, although it's much more labor-intensive, I laser print each envelope, rather than use address labels. And I apply individual self-adhesive stamps instead of using a postal meter. Bulk mail is all right for *self-mailers*, which are single-sheet promotions that are folded and mailed without envelopes. But for letters, I've found that the personal touch gets more attention, which is the point, after all.

Remember, too, that one of the basic tenets of direct mail is that it needs to be sent on a regular basis in order to build name recognition and credibility over a period of time. Persistence is a success characteristic that everyone with a message must buy into, regardless of the business you're in. To quote Mary Matalin, former Republican party political director, "the absolute rule of message dissemination and message penetration is consistency and repetition. This principle is the same for political campaigns or companies."

If you send out a mailing and get a disappointing return, don't give up. Make the necessary adjustments and keep on mailing.

Direct Mail Hygiene

To ensure that the mail you send creates an impact, not a landfill, try to observe the following rules of list maintenance:

- **Build your list** by continually adding fresh names. Otherwise, you'll wear out your welcome and your list will become stale.

- **Clean your list** by removing duplicated names, deleting unwanted names, correcting the spellings of names (misspelled names are a huge turnoff to prospects) and adjusting or deleting names in response to a relocation. This ongoing process is called list hygiene in the trade, and it's one of the most important canons of direct mail.

- **Test your list** by sending out mail to a small sample portion at first. If you get a bad return, drop the list or make other adjustments before you send more money down a bottomless pit. If you get a favorable response, then you know your investment is going to pay off, and you can crank the mailing up to full volume. Generally speaking, a test list should consist of at least 500 to 1,000 pieces. Anything less would be statistically invalid.

- **Code or document your list.** Otherwise, you may not be able to identify which message works best, or which set of customers you're getting your returns from.

- **Track the success of your list.** I generate a printout for every mailing and keep score of all the inquiries, returns (the non-deliverable pieces that need to be corrected or purged) and invoices that are tied to the mailing.

By adding "address correction requested" to the return address on your envelope, you'll instruct the post office to provide you with any changes in the recipient's address. This technique can save you time when cleaning your list.

Systematic Mailing Cycles

In my business, I've settled on a three-times-a-year rotation for each company, with regular mailings going out each month. My system divides prospects into four monthly code groups, starting with "11" (first quarter/first month, or

January), "12" (first quarter/second month, or February), and so on.

Mail code	Month	Month	Month	Totals
A	1100 (Jan)	2200 (May)	3300 (Sept)	
# pieces	350	200	450	1000
B	1200 (Feb)	2300 (June)	4100 (Oct)	
# pieces	300	200	500	1000
C	1300 (March)	3100 (July)	4200 (Nov)	
# pieces	375	225	400	1000
D	2100 (April)	3200 (Aug)	4300 (Dec)	
# pieces	240	400	360	1000

By following this formula, I'll send out 1000 letters a month from mail codes A, B, C or D. So a company that's designated "22" (May) will get my letters three times a year, in January, May and September. The reason I developed monthly codes was so I could add to the list each month and still keep track of when a new prospect was added.

Since recruiting is essentially a non-seasonal business (unlike retail or catalog marketing, for example), there's no good or bad month to send a mailing. However, common sense dictates that you avoid holidays or industry-specific crunch times (like tax season, for example, if you work an accounting desk) as your target receiving date. The best day of the week to mail is Friday; the prospect will receive the letter at midweek, rather than on a Monday or a Friday, the two days I consider to be bad for mail reading.

Hillary, Rush and O.J.

Although direct mail pieces can vary considerably, all strong pieces have these four features in common:

[1] A piece must be attractive and easy to understand. The last thing you want is for the prospect (who you spent so much time and effort trying to reach) to puzzle over the piece of mail in his hand and not "get it." Whether the piece is a postcard, a self-mailer, a letter, an insert, a catalog or a glossy brochure, your message should run as clear as a trout stream in Alaska.

[2] A piece should have a "hook" or attention grabber. This is an opening sentence or phrase that compels the prospect to continue reading (if it's a letter); or open the piece and read what's inside (if it's a self-mailed brochure or there's a message on your envelope).

Your hook, in order to grab attention, needs to "pinch" the prospect by appealing to his or her desire for gain or fear of loss. While a hook like "What do Hillary, Rush and O.J. have in common?"(a hook I almost mailed to 800 prospects before sanity kicked in) may get attention, it has nothing to do with an employer's hiring needs.

However, a hook like, "How much money did you lose last quarter from poor quality products?" speaks more to the needs of the prospect, and is much more likely to generate a response.

Make your hook as interesting as possible. As the old saying goes, "You can't bore someone into buying."

[3] A piece has to offer the prospect several benefits for responding. Here's where your skill in selling really pays off. If you can get inside the needs of

the prospect and offer a solution, then your message is strong, and you'll get back a positive response. This exercise should be a snap, since you're already a pro at scripting benefit statements from your cold calling. Right?

[4] A piece must demand the prospect's participation in a call to action. "Call me today toll-free" or "Simply drop our postage-paid response card in the mail for more information" are a couple of the clichés of the trade commonly used to mobilize the prospect. You want to make it as easy as possible for the prospect to reach you.

P.S. It's been shown that a "P.S." is read by nearly 80 percent of all direct mail recipients. Don't overlook this powerful attention grabber as a sales tool.

Direct Mail Letters: Scripting the Offer

There are several different types of letters you can write to generate new business, depending on what you have to offer:

- **Service letters** describe your unique capabilities for servicing the specific staffing needs of your target population. These letters require a powerful hook and a compelling reason why you're the best in the business.

- **Hot candidate letters** are the written equivalent to the MPA or "most placeable applicant" style of cold call, and should be formatted to bullet-point the most salable features of a candidate. You may want to enclose a coded resume, but you run the risk of making your letter look like just another unsolicited attempt by an unemployed candidate to find a job.

- **Talent scout letters** provide a snapshot of a group of high-quality candidates that can be perused by the prospect. The trick is to provide a nice spread of most placeable talent, but within the specific target market you're trying to penetrate.

- **EIO (employer in office) letters** are a variation on the talent scout letter. Simply put, you let the prospect know that he or she is invited to a staffing center you're sponsoring at your office (or at the local Marriott or wherever) with five talented candidates, any one of which, when hired by the prospect, would be capable of increasing productivity (designing new products, expanding market share, etc.) for the prospect's company.

- **Congratulatory letters** acknowledge a specific event or action taken by the prospect or his company, such as a promotion, a new product introduction, a merger, or the creation of a new position.

- **Article response letters** are sent to the people in your industry whose articles have recently appeared in trade magazines or association newsletters.

Each of these types of letters has its niche in terms of purpose and expected return. While a more highly focused letter (such as an announcement letter) may have a better chance of a return, it would be impractical to send as many of these types of letters as it would be the more generic letters, such as the service letter. Since all letters have their merits, I would suggest using the full range of weapons in your arsenal.

For example, the biggest payoff I ever got came from the type of letter least likely (from a statistical standpoint) to generate a response.

By dashing off a stock article response letter, I piqued the curiosity of a sales and marketing vice president who just happened to be in need of several key people. He called me a couple of days after receiving my letter, and his company became one of my biggest clients.

In terms of style and format, my theory is that if you write a letter, you should keep it to a single page and write with short, clear sentences and paragraphs. In other words, provide plenty of blank space so as not to overwhelm the prospect with a lot of verbiage.

How to Measure Success

Naturally, the quality and rate of response you get will vary, depending on your offer. If you're marketing your service, you may receive an inquiry for generic information that will be filed by the prospect for later reference; or you may receive an inquiry regarding your fees or specialization. If you're marketing a candidate via direct mail, then you may get a request for additional candidate information or a schedule check to set up an interview.

I measure my initial response rate by the number of inquiries I receive from a mailing, not the number of sales that ultimately result from the inquiries. If you think of inquiries as being like sendouts, then you'll recognize that the greater the number you put into the top of the funnel, the greater your chance for success.

As in the case of sendouts, numbers alone can't guarantee a payoff. That's why you should always look for ways to improve your rate of closure on inquiries. By delivering a strong presentation of your benefits to the customer and providing a well-organized and effective set of support materials, you'll stand a good chance of capturing the order.

Recruiters operate in a big-ticket, slow selling cycle world (the higher the level of candidate, the slower the sale), in which it's difficult to track direct mail marketing on a one-to-one or time-bounded basis. So even if your piece is designed to trigger an immediate response, don't be surprised if you receive an inquiry from a prospect several months after a mailing.

Pay close attention to the message you send. Unless you have something specific to sell, and can communicate the benefits with a sense of urgency, you're not using direct mail to its best advantage. Sure, you can send out a newsletter or a flyer announcing your recent promotion or address change, but what's the point?

Running, Throwing and Punting

Orchestrating a direct mail campaign is kind of like coaching the offense of a football team. If running up the middle doesn't work against the defense, try running wide. If that doesn't work, try throwing the ball.

If throwing the ball works, keep doing it. Over and over, until it no longer works. Then try something else.

My first direct mail campaign was a complete disaster, probably because it was flawed in each of the essential areas we've discussed. Using the football analogy, I was tackled behind the line of scrimmage, and had to punt. The only response I got was from an HR manager who felt the need to call me to point out that the letter inside the envelope he received was addressed to someone at a different company.

Besides screwing up my letter stuffing, I found out that my list management wasn't all that great. Not only was the list too small to begin with, but of the 350 letters I sent, many were sent to different people in the same company, so I ended up wasting about 100 letters and diminishing the pool of prospective customers. (It's like Victoria's Secret sending three catalogs to each household.) The prospects who received my message ranged from engineers to sales managers to HR managers to presidents; in other words, they were all over the map.

In terms of the piece, I wrote a hook I thought was a real attention grabber. My letter began with the line,

> *Okay, admit it. Trying to fill a key position is about as much fun as having your rented Winnebago break down in the middle of Manitoba, right?*

What was I possibly thinking? That a little "humor" would compel the prospect to pick up the phone and give me a search assignment?

The Winnebago letter was the biggest blunder I ever made with respect to direct mail. The letter was complicated, tried to sell the prospect on every conceivable point, and made its first benefit statement only after annoying the reader half to death. Just thinking about the letter now makes me cringe.

Finding the Right Combination

Another mistake I made with the Winnebago letter was to send a letter and a business card, instead of a letter and a brochure, which is what I send now. The letter/card format, I'm afraid, was totally ineffective.

Business cards don't add credibility, sell anything or build a strong case for using an expensive service. Including a business card with the letter just gives the prospect more paper products to throw away.

So I replaced the business card with a brochure, and now I'm getting a solid two percent return. (Of course, my list and my piece have also been substantially improved.) A letter and a brochure sent together will strengthen the overall offer, in that the letter acts as a grabber, and the brochure provides information that supports the letter.

I've also tried just the brochure as a self-mailer, but it lacked a "hook" or any sense of urgency. Brochures by themselves are usually too dry and non-specific in their focus to have much impact. They really need a letter as a personalized form of introduction.

If you don't have the budget for a brochure, a suitable alternative is a single page insert that describes the benefits of your service or your unique background. And unless price is a big selling point (which is hardly ever the case, except in the temporary placement business in which margins often make the difference), don't include a fee schedule. Your objective is to emphasize value, not cost.

The direct mail approach to marketing takes time and a bit of practice to develop, but the payback is well worth the investment.

Start with the list of prospects you already have, and add to it so you mail to a minimum of 300 or 400 prospects. If you don't get results at first, look at what might have gone wrong and make the necessary adjustments.

Marcom and Your Business Identity

Just as the telephone, computer, fax machine and copier represent the essential tools of your trade, so are the written materials that collectively telegraph your unique business identity to your customers.

Known as marketing communications (or marcom for short), these items, if carefully designed, can distinguish you from the competition and reinforce your position within your constituency.

Naturally, the stylistic characteristics of your marketing materials will vary, depending on your budget and the message you're trying to get across. Basic materials for recruiters include:

- **Stationery, business cards and address labels.**
  These should look professional, project a successful image, and fit comfortably within the expectations of your target market.

- **Logo design.** Here again, your logo should conform to the general tastes of your industry. If you work with high tech companies, for example, you might want a space-age logo; if you deal with the hospitality industry, something flashy might work well. Or, if your constituency is the legal profession, a subdued approach to marcom might best fall within your clients' comfort zone.

- **Brochures.** These can range from simple one-color 8.5x11 *trifolds* to customized four-color works of art. For a really slick brochure, you'll probably need to work with an ad agency, unless you can find a freelancer who's capable of grasping exactly what you do for a living (which is pretty unlikely).

- **Custom presentation folders.** Like brochures, these can either be foil stamped and printed on prefabricated stock, or designed by an ad agency for maximum visual impact. Presentation folders make perfect "kits" that can be filled with contracts, brochures, reprints, and so forth.

- **Professional profiles and service descriptions.** These can be laser-printed onto your company stationery and placed inside your presentation folder.

- **Inserts.** Designed to fit in a business envelope, 4x9 inserts describe the benefits of your service and provide a brief professional biography.

- **Professional references.** The names and numbers of past clients can be printed onto your stationery and placed in your presentation folder.

- **Testimonials.** These "love letters" from happy customers should be written on your clients' letterhead, and photocopied or bound together.

- **Value-added materials or "freebies."** These are brochures, inserts or reprints that supply useful (or self-serving) information to your constituents. Many specialized search firms, for example, provide annual industry-specific salary surveys to their candidates, or reprint current articles that may be of interest to employers.

Although the importance of these types of materials cannot be overestimated, you have to decide how much money you need to invest in order for them to be effective.

I would rate the materials I use as functional and minimally slick. I haven't yet found it necessary to hire an ad agency to create materials that I can develop on my own. With the help of my PowerBook, an ancient PageMaker program and a laser printer, I've been able to home-grow the marcom I need, and exercise the flexibility to make modifications whenever I feel they're necessary.

Advertising and Public Relations

As I mentioned earlier, I placed an article with a niche-market trade magazine that directly resulted in increased candidate flow, industry notoriety and ultimately, $30,000 in billings.

I never consciously set out to become a writer; stringing together a bunch of words is just something I've learned to do out of necessity. I've found that as long as I have something to say (and a literate friend or relative who can do a little proofreading), there's no reason I can't produce perfectly adequate articles or editorials --- and reap the benefits of my newfound fame.

If you feel your writing skills are weak (or you simply don't have the time), you can hire a ghostwriter on a work-for-hire basis to craft an article with your byline.

To make serious waves, you can retain a publicist to assist you in what's called *media placement*, which covers everything from a write-up in the business section of your local newspaper to an appearance on Donahue (I can see it now: "Recruiters who sleep with their modems").

Your visibility can also be enhanced whenever you send a newsletter to clients, speak at a trade show, or sponsor a technical or business seminar for the edification of your constituency. By using a little creativity, you'll be surprised by how much advertising you can generate, most of it for hardly any effort or expense.

Revise and Enhance
Your Written Communications

I'm sure that most, if not all, of your written materials are serving you well. In fact, it wouldn't surprise me if your letters, brochures, contracts and internal communications are more effective than mine.

However, assuming there's room for improvement or the implementation of an idea or two, please feel free to copy, rewrite or modify any of the written materials I've used as examples in the book for your own use.

Throughout *Shut Up and Make More Money*, I've avoided the temptation to pick apart and explain each and every one of the examples. Everything, I think, is pretty much self-explanatory, and it's certainly not my goal to give you eyestrain or expect you to obsess over every comma, colon or ampersand.

I've really enjoyed sharing some of my experiences with you. The truth is, I love this business, and I really want to help people succeed. If *Shut Up and Make More Money* in some small way delivers what it promises, then we'll both be better off --- I'll have gotten a kick from imparting my knowledge; and you'll continue to grow as a useful and productive member of our dynamic and ever-evolving employment market.

Which is, after all, the point.

Good luck, and happy headhunting!

Fig. 13.1 A hot candidate letter is the written equivalent of an MPA call.

January 5, 1995

Mr. Brian Jones
Managing Director
FISH HEAD SENSORS
King Henry's Drive
New Addington
Croydon CR9 OBG
ENGLAND

Dear Mr. Jones:

Since our last correspondence, my executive search firm has been engaged in an exclusive search assignment for a president of a medium-sized high-tech company with products similar to yours.

One of the candidates we surfaced has an outstanding background as president/CEO of a company that designs and manufactures sensor and instrumentation products (including a highly profitable nuclear-safety-qualified pressure transmitter), and may very well be suited to one of your North American divisions.

Enclosed is his resume for your perusal. Please let me know if this candidate meets your requirements.

Sincerely,

William G. Radin, president
RADIN ASSOCIATES

WGR: rbl

Enclosure

Fig. 13.2 If sent on a regular basis, service letters can be extremely effective.

September 16, 1994

Mr. Bruce Koll
ALLEN-BRADLEY COMPANY, INC.
1201 S. Second Street
Milwaukee, WI 53204

Dear Mr. Koll:

Pop Quiz: Name your three worst sales engineers.

... and think of the tens, even hundreds of thousands of dollars you're *losing* each year from inadequate sales coverage.

Why do you keep them? Is it because you don't think you can find better replacements? No surprise to us. Over half the people we recommend to our clients never read the Sunday classifieds --- they're too busy making sales calls to bother with a job search!

So why wait to hire up the best sales engineers?

Radin Associates can help you turn weak sales territories into *huge profit centers* by finding the best people in the business. Call me today at (505) 983-2243 to discuss how we can help turn missed opportunities into bottom-line dollars for your company.

Sincerely,

William G. Radin, president
RADIN ASSOCIATES

WGR: rbl / Enclosure

P.S. Looking to penetrate or increase your sales volume in the Asian marketplace? We can help enhance your presence in Pacific Rim countries such as Japan, mainland China, Thailand and Malaysia. Call today for details!

Fig. 13.3 An article response letter landed one of my largest accounts.

February 10, 1995

Mr. John C. Smith
SCIENTIFIC DESIGNS, INC.
1445 NW Mall Street
Spokane, WA 98027-5344

Dear Mr. Smith:

Your article in the January issue of *SENSORS* magazine reminded me that a product has absolutely *no value* unless it can be sold to the end user.

Through our unique program, however, we can help you *increase sales* by identifying the top-producing sales engineers that cover your customer base. As experienced executive recruiters specializing in the sensor industry, we know how to reach the decision-makers who buy your products in a given territory and find out who they consider to be *the best sales engineers in the business.*

By utilizing this direct-referral methodology plus other networking and cross-referencing techniques, we can quickly and accurately construct a matrix of high-performing sales engineers according to the *exact parameters you define* as critical to success.

Since sales performance is of paramount importance in a competitive market, we urge you to consider our *proven approach* to sales engineering sourcing. Please call me today at (505) 983-2243 to discuss your company's specific requirements.

Sincerely,

William G. Radin, president
RADIN ASSOCIATES

WGR: rbl
Enclosure

Fig. 13.4 This trifold brochure was used as both an insert and a self-mailer.

Radin
Associates

Executive
Search
Services

©1995 Radin Associates

Research Capabilities

Our first line of research consists of a CD-ROM-accessible database that accurately profiles over 8,000,000 U.S. companies. The Radin Associates library also contains a full complement of current industrial directories, product catalogs, annual reports and market-specific trade, scientific and association publications. And our extensive network of industry contacts developed through years of sensor and instrumentation consulting gives us the edge when it comes to identifying key individuals in critical market segments.

The Sensor Specialists

• William G. Radin, president, held the position of Manager of Sensor Technologies at Search West, Inc. prior to founding Radin Associates. A member of the Instrument Society of America and the International Society of Weighing and Measurement, Mr. Radin earned an MA in liberal arts from the University of Southern California and a BA from the University of Cincinnati. His guest columns have appeared in *Weighing & Measurement* and *SENSORS* magazines.

• William H. Moss, consultant, was formerly VP of Marketing for Computer Products, Inc., and was responsible for sales and marketing management and applications engineering for the Hudson Products and Bailey Controls divisions of McDermott International. Mr. Moss is a registered engineer and holds an MBA and an MS in Chemical Engineering from Case Western Reserve University and a BS in Chemical Engineering from the Case Institute of Technology.

 Radin Associates

2373 Brother Abdon Way, Santa Fe, New Mexico 87505
VOICE (505) 983-2243 • FAX (505) 983-2244

Consultants in Executive Search

Your Organization Needs the Competitive Advantage

Fact: Your company's ability to compete in a global economy will depend on the expertise of your staff, and how well they can establish new markets, exploit innovative technologies, and implement evolving manufacturing capabilities. In other words, *your organization can only be as strong as the talent within.*

Of course, this begs the question: Where will these key contributors come from? The answer may lie somewhere within your own organization — or it may not. At some point, most companies find that they must recruit from the outside to acquire the proven technical skills or managerial leadership they need in order to grow and prosper.

Helping You Harness the Power of Human Potential

Since 1985, Radin Associates has played a vital role in bringing together significant players within the sensor and instrumentation industries. As niche-market specialists, we know how to find the high-achieving individuals you need and attract them to your company.

We can help your organization build a powerful team that creates original designs and inspires increased productivity. Whether your needs are in research, product development, quality assurance, sales, manufacturing or general management, we firmly believe that any search for excellence must first begin with excellence in search.

A Reputation for Excellence in the Sensor & Instrumentation Markets

Over the years, we've helped a sizeable number of highly respected companies in the sensor and instrumentation industries locate and secure the best available talent. Our clients include:

(*Sensors*)
Barksdale Controls
CEC Instruments
Endevco, Inc.
G.L. Collins Corporation
Lake Shore Cryotronics, Inc.
MagneTek Transducers
Micro Gage, Inc.
Sensortronics, Inc.
Spectrol Electronics
Tayco Engineering
Thermocontrol, Inc.
Toledo Transducers, Inc.
TransLogic, Inc.
TRW Vehicle Safety Systems

(*Instruments*)
Computer Products, Inc.
MDT Corporation
Metra Corporation
NBC North America
Pesa Scale, Inc
PMI Food Equipment Group
Toledo Scale

Our Goal: To Find You the Best People in the Business

Helping your organization achieve its potential is our highest priority. As executive recruiters specializing in the sensor and instrumentation markets, we have what it takes to find best people in the business!

Our Proven Approach to Executive Search

Our experience has shown that the process of attracting top industry talent consists of three distinct phases:

[1] *Recruit* — We begin by identifying individuals who possess the technical and motivational qualifications you require. After careful screening, we then schedule face-to-face interviews with the most highly qualified candidates.

[2] *Offer* — After mutual interest is determined, we assist in negotiating an acceptable compensation package with the finalist you select.

[3] *Transition* — Once your offer is formally accepted, we help provide for a smooth transfer to your company, by counselling the new hire on proper resignation procedures and by helping to facilitate the move.

A Comprehensive Service That Saves You Time and Energy

At Radin Associates, we go the extra mile to ensure that qualified candidates are signed, sealed, and delivered. After all, the last thing you need is to waste your time and energy with people who have no sincere interest in changing jobs or who have a history of turning down good faith offers of employment.

To ensure that candidates are selected for both technical merit and motivational suitability, our screening process includes reference checking, degree verification, and if required, psychometric testing.

Fig. 13.5 A written, signed testimonial is worth its weight in gold.

AUTOMOTIVE SYSTEMS LABORATORY, INC.
27200 Haggerty Road Suite B-12
Farmington Hills, Michigan 48331

313/489-5930

November 29, 1989

TO WHOM IT MAY CONCERN:

While at TRW I had the pleasure of working with Mr. William G. Radin on a search for an electronic sensor engineer for a new electronic crash sensor program at TRW. The center of excellence for this sensor technology is in California and it is very difficult to find an engineer who would be willing to move to the cold midwest/Detroit.

Mr. Radin accepted the challenge and identified the companies who were leaders in electronic sensor development and subsequently identified a candidate who we interviewed, checked references on. We subsequently made an offer to him and he joined TRW.

The candidate has since become the leader of the sensor development team at TRW.

Mr. Radin is extremely thorough in identifying the key requirements for the candidate and performs an excellent pre-screening interview to ensure no false starts. Mr. Radin also has that rare characteristic these days which is a sense of urgency to get the job done. He also remembers to follow up to ensure that details do not fall through the cracks.

Mr. Radin does not disappoint the customer. I recommend him highly.

Yours Truly,

Joseph F. Ziomek

Joseph F. Ziomek
Dir. of Technology Assessment

About the Author

BILL RADIN began his career in executive search in 1985, after receiving his masters degree from the University of Southern California.

As a specialist in the permanent placement of electrical engineers, Bill quickly established himself as a top-producing recruiter and department manager, serving the needs of a wide range of client companies, including such multinational giants as TRW, Westinghouse and Emerson Electric.

Under his leadership as training director, Bill helped Search West of Los Angeles and Management Recruiters of Cincinnati set individual and company billing records.

By combining years of practical recruiting and management experience with modern selling technology, Bill's innovative training methods have helped produce dramatic, measurable performance improvements in both new and experienced recruiters.

He is the founder of Innovative Consulting, a company dedicated to the growth and development of the executive search industry, and continues his full-time search activities as president of Radin Associates.

Bill resides in Cincinnati, Ohio with his wife Ruth.

Index

ORDER FORM
Books and Tapes by Bill Radin

Please rush:

___ *How to Market & Sell Your Recruiting Services* @ $79.95 $ _____

___ *How to Write High-Profit Job Orders* @ $79.95 $ _____

___ *Time Management Secrets of Top-Producing Recruiters* @ $79.95 $ _____

___ *Billing Power!* @ $49.95 $ _____

___ *The Recruiter's Almanac* @ $49.95 $ _____

___ *Shut Up & Make More Money* @ $49.95 $ _____

___ *Career Development Reports* @ $49.95 $ _____

___ *Recruiting & The Art of Control* @ $195.00 $ _____

      Subtotal $ _____

      Less 15% for orders of 3 or more products *(any combination)* $ _____

      Add $5.00 shipping & handling $ _____

      GRAND TOTAL $ _____

Name _____

Company _____

Street _____

City _____ State _____

Zip _____ Telephone _____

Payment: _____ Check _____ Visa/MC _____ Discover _____ AMEX

Card number _____ Exp. _____

Signature _____

Call toll-free or fax to: (800) 837-7224 • Fax: (513) 624-7502

Order online at: www.billradin.com

Or send to: INNOVATIVE CONSULTING, INC.
                5193 Adena Trail, Cincinnati, Ohio 45230